COMING HOME

COMING HOME

SARA WENGER SHENK

Good Books

Intercourse, PA 17534

Design by Dawn J. Ranck

Cover photograph by Edwin P. Huddle

Those biblical citations given as "NRSV" are from the New Revised Standard Version Bible, copyright © 1989, by the Division of Christian Education of the National Council of Churches of Christ in the United States of America. Used by permission.

COMING HOME
Copyright © 1992 by Good Books, Intercourse, PA 17534
International Standard Book Number: 1-56148-060-6
Library of Congress Catalog Card Number: 92-12601

Library of Congress Cataloging-in-Publication Data

Shenk, Sara Wenger, 1953-
    Coming home : a thoughtful resource for fathers, mothers, and the
    rebirth of the family / Sara Wenger Shenk.
        p.   cm.
    Includes bibliographical references.
    ISBN 1-56148-060-6 : $9.95
    1. Family—United States. 2. Family—Religious life.
3. Parenting—United States. I. Title.
HQ536.S483   1992
306.85'0973—dc20

                                    92-12601
                                        CIP

Printed on recycled paper stock.

Table of Contents

Preface

After a generation and more of messages, subtle and blatant, that the real action is "out there" somewhere, the home has come to resemble a burned-out shell. Exaggerated image, I know! But think about it. When our best energies are spent elsewhere, the creative core of home life is consumed, as if by fire. What remains is an unsightly shell, a mockery of shelter, a fragile frame. Family life "as it used to be" takes on mythic proportions as we grope for its fleeting memories. Even many family artifacts, diaries and photographs are lost. They now belong to another irretrievable era.

If we hope to restore life together, its character has to be radically reconceived. A rebirth of color, fragrance, warmth and laughter between the burned-out walls will require heroic effort and lavish grace. From where will we find the courage to start over? Bursts of inspiration must first rekindle the will to begin again. And then, a vision of resurrection, pulsating with life, may capture our imaginations.

It is that vision of life together, reconceived and resurrected, that I hope to inspire in these meditations. Most of the homes I know intimately are not gutted by fire. Yet each of us is constantly battling flames that threaten to consume what we had hoped might characterize our life together.

Last week our family of five sat as guests at the table of a family from India. Anil, a colleague of Gerald's at the seminary, had invited us for an authentic rice and curry feast. We savored the aroma that greeted us at the door. The fellowship and delectable food ministered to spirits and bodies. Tears welled unnoticed in my eyes. My life had recently spiraled out of control. The opportunity to sit unhurried at a table with dear friends shone with a rare luster. It had been too long. The business of everyday life and all that I normally cram into it had crowded out shimmering moments. I mourned their loss.

The death of shimmering moments is not a sudden one. Death

creeps in gradually, unannounced. It stifles the spirit slowly, breath by breath. Unless (bless God), unless a shimmering moment catches us off guard, and we weep—weep for all the times we were too busy to care, for all the moments that could have been. Unless we determine once again to structure our lives so as to make space for grace in the hearts of our homes.

Grace would have it that a few days after the Indian meal, a group gathered in our living room for a Sunday fellowship meal. We'd expected to hold it at church, but because the group was unusually small, we invited them home. It was another shimmering moment, a time for unhooking from established routines, simply to be together. The potluck-style meal was delightfully balanced. Conversation flowed easily among adults and children. Greta, our three-year-old, insisted that I bring in all eight of our new baby rabbits. After she and a friend played with them for a while in a big box in the middle of the living room, she proceeded, as if inspired, to pass them out one by one to the gathered group. The picture of that circle of adults (professionals, students, homemakers) each cuddling a tiny soft rabbit even while carrying on some rather serious conversation, will long remain in my mind.

Coming Home is about commitment to each other. And more than that, it is about a passion for preserving the center of what sustains us as human beings. That center is life together. Our homes are the cradle of life together. And where two or three are gathered in Jesus' name, there, inexplicably, is the Source of all that is good.

— Sara Wenger Shenk
Harrisonburg, Virginia

I.

Revolution of Hope at Home

1.
Simple Pleasures

It was an ordinary weekday evening, but the meal was festive. To commemorate my husband Gerald's completion of a difficult writing project, I had prepared two simple and highly spiced Ethiopian dishes for supper. Our sons were pleased that Dad had met his deadline, and even more delighted to rip off pieces of flat pancake-like *injera* and dip them into the red-hot stew.

While dousing flames in his mouth with great gulps of water, our six-year-old remarked, "I can't believe it! Just the simplest things at home can be so exciting!" I sank back into my chair for a quiet moment of exultation. Gerald's eyes shone across the table.

Our family likes to celebrate—not with a lot of fanfare—but by deliberately marking and enriching moments in time. It's an art we are cultivating after watching too much time slip through our fingers in a frantic blur. On any ordinary day, there are far too few hallowed moments, particularly in our homes; too few occasions to savor time-honored stories with our children; too few gestures of old-fashioned hospitality; too few festive activities to send our spirits soaring.

The year after our daughter was born put a severe strain on my stock of survival skills. No falling asleep at the breast for this champion wrestler. She needed to be jogged, and that rather energetically, before she surrendered to slumber—and then sleep seemed just an excuse to waken again.

Would we trade her to a gypsy for a nickel? Only in jest. But day after day she sucked life out of me. And our extended family was an ocean away.

I remember shaking with sobs one day after reading a well-written article. The beauty of the piece pierced me, but more than that, I suddenly realized how eternally long it seemed since I had written a word.

Can I say it, without sounding melodramatic, that this toughest of years was also the most fulfilling? I am given to murmuring on the ragged edges of many days, but nearly every day there are moments when I swell fit to burst with the joy of being with these little people. They truly have remade me, turning a heart of arrogance into a throbbing heart of tenderness. And they continue to convert me day after day toward simple pleasures amid the hurly-burly. The fun, food and companionship we share with them and others are surrounding us with a cloak of security, with rhyme and reason, with anticipation and fulfillment, over and over again.

We desperately need a revolution of hope at home—a revolution of celebration! With children who thrive on simple pleasures, our work and our entire society can be renewed.

2.
Talking about Parenting is Dangerous

I told someone the other day that just as Gerald and I are being asked more often to speak on parenting, I feel that I'm losing my nerve. The challenges of adjusting to a newborn's unending demands pale in comparison to the wisdom, diplomacy and humility required to gracefully maneuver the teen years. Yet even as I owned my anxiety, the prospect of helping to steer a clear course through all the confusion of the current teen scene is a thrill, particularly as it calls us to account more explicitly for our own walk of faith.

Even so, it takes a lot of nerve to expound knowingly on the how-to's of parenting. Anyone in the middle of it is made fully aware every day how little anyone actually knows about it. Those of us submerged in parenting wonder every day how to do it. Parenting is one of the most awesome responsibilities imaginable. There is no guaranteed outcome. No victories are final. There are no formulas for success. Each of our homes has more failures than any of us wants to admit.

Talking about parenting is one of the easiest things to do since being a parent makes up such a gigantic part of every day's doings. But it is also one of the toughest things to talk about because it's so slippery, so unmeasurable in its outcomes. The subject matter is our most intimate relationships where people know us in the raw.

Worthy and necessary as the many manuals on good parenting techniques are, it isn't the how-to's that grip my imagination. It is, instead, the spirit, the joy, the vision of a family life where the love of God can flourish. There is something contagious about a family that celebrates the whole of life. A family with an inner dynamism of joy and forgiveness generates life that ripples outward in a way that includes many others.

There is something truly miraculous about a family that works, an undefinable quality that causes people to wonder—how can it be that good? Such families make a lot of us uneasy because our own approximations of the ideal look that much more impoverished by comparison. After what was meant to be an inspiring weekend on parenting for peace and justice led by a well-known husband-wife team, one participant remarked to me with heaviness in her voice, "There were so many good ideas but where does one find the time or energy to bring them to life?" Rather than an inspiration, the vision of all-that-could-be had left a residue of despair.

It is always a dilemma in discussions of marriage and family life—does one hold up the vision of the ideal marital relationship and a flourishing family, when the truth is that none of us is able to realize them as fully as we'd like?

Without a vision, we perish! We are inspired by the vision of perfection even though we know it is beyond us. W. A. Visser t'Hooft remarked that when partners in a genuine marriage remain faithful to each other it is not primarily because of the rules—but because they don't want to lose or spoil a relationship that is their greatest blessing. A marriage where both *eros* and *agape* find their place is the most precious human relationship. It is time to speak, he said, of marriages where men and women, with deep gratitude, have found each other, and having done so, covenant together that at all cost they will guard that relationship (Visser t' Hooft, 1982, p. 52).

The time is here to speak, humbly but unapologetically, of the grand adventure it is to be in family, celebrating the bonds of affection that sustain us and free us to grow in grace and in the knowledge and love of God.

And it *is* grace that allows us to keep the vision alive without being completely unnerved by its color and vitality. Grace sustains us even through failure, even when our best efforts seem to come to nothing. And love undergirds. Garrison Keillor, in one of his compelling stories, concludes: "Love has brought a lot of people to safety when competence is exhausted, even the competence of fathers."

3.
Parenting as Spiritual Discipline

The grand illusion flagrantly paraded in our generation has been that you can have it all. The birth of a child represents a major disruption for an upwardly mobile young couple—if they intend to take the needs of the child seriously. The baby's rhythms, the baby's desire to cuddle and cling all demand sacrifices from her parents if they want to have a significant relationship with her. Babies can't be programmed to the fast track. They don't wait for convenient moments to be fed and diapered. They don't thrive with only perfunctory hugs and leftover affection.

Babies don't ask to be born. Nor do they promise to fit into our lifestyle. They simply *are*. In their weakness, they compel us toward costly choices that go against all that we've been programmed to expect for ourselves.

And babies don't go away. They grow into little people who continue to need us, to implore us to stay home, to not go away to so many meetings; they beg us to play with them, to wipe their tears and bandage their knees, to tuck them into bed and sing away their fears. They need our time, our affection, our devotion to their cause. Their eyes and entire bodies cry out: SLOW DOWN and tell us even just occasionally that we matter.

Jesus said, "Whoever welcomes a little child like this in my name welcomes me." He implies that whoever refuses to welcome a child rejects Jesus and the One who sent him. In fact, to harm a child in any way, even to look down on a child in a disparaging manner is tantamount to cutting oneself off from God. It would be better for such a person "to have a large millstone hung around his neck and to be drowned in the depths of the sea" (Matthew 18: 2-10, NIV). Jesus minces no words when he defends children.

One hears a lot of talk in some circles about spiritual disciplines like prayer, fasting, meditation and simplicity. Another discipline could be added to the list: parenting. If we care for our children as Jesus would, it becomes a profound, life-changing discipline of the spirit. There is perhaps no more significant sign that one is a disciple of Jesus Christ than one's welcome with a tender, caring heart for children. Parenting, at least for most of us, requires a commitment to downward mobility. Every aspect of our lives is affected if we take parenting seriously. We simplify our schedules and lifestyles. Our paychecks don't go nearly as far. Our priorities reflect relationships above career advancements. Our commitments are toward the wellbeing of children, not an unquestioning support of an American "way of life." There is a Navajo saying that a man can't get rich if he takes proper care of his family.

Last summer on our family vacation we spent some time at the Grand Canyon enroute to a church general assembly. While hiking along the South Rim of the canyon we stopped at a souvenir shop to buy a hat for one of the boys. The sun's heat was intense. Two mothers with an assortment of children sat waiting for their husbands on the store veranda. We heard a lot of: "Carla, get down off that wall!" and "Brent, would you quit climbing all over me!" and "Cut it out, you two. Leave each other alone!" In the midst of it all one mother remarked to the other, "Next year we're leaving the children at home. They've been nothing but a pain. . ." There was a commiserating nod and more complaining. I looked with sympathy on the lively little ones and was grateful to see one of the fathers emerge from the store. He stooped down, picked up a child and spoke kindly to her. "Come on, let's go," he called. All is not lost, I thought.

Children are a pain! They endlessly complicate life. But it's not *their* fault. It's our unrealistic expectations and *our* inability as parents to achieve some rapport with them. To embrace parenting as a spiritual discipline is to put children first for a season. It doesn't mean doting on them as the ultimate meaning of our existence. Nor does it mean turning them into showcase models of our excellent parenting. We put them first because they come to us as Christ did, weak and vulnerable. Christ comes to us in and through them. In serving them we have unparalleled opportunities to grow in the knowledge and grace of Jesus Christ himself.

Any spiritual discipline has its costs, but there are also immeasurable benefits. Devotion to the well-being of children will be rewarded one hundredfold. The beauty within each of them will blossom in time with fragrance and color. My grandmother, who was never wealthy, sophisticated or highly educated, used to smile the most beatific smile of contentment. Speaking, I think, of both her spiritual and her biological children, she would say, "There is *no greater reward* than to see my children walk in truth." And I believe her.

II.

In the Wilderness, Lost and Homeless

4.
Take Us Back to Egypt

The Israelites groaned in their slavery and cried out, and their cry for help because of their slavery went up to God. God heard their groaning and he remembered his covenant with Abraham, with Isaac and with Jacob. So God looked on the Israelites and was concerned about them.

In the desert the whole community grumbled against Moses and Aaron. The Israelites said to them, "If only we had died by the Lord's hand in Egypt! There we sat around pots of meat and ate all the food we wanted, but you have brought us out into this desert to starve this entire assembly to death."

(Exodus 2:23-25, 16:2-3, NIV)

A family discussion among grown siblings touched some raw nerves. Before I knew it, what had been a calm, thoughtful theological discussion turned emotional. Some hot buttons were pushed. Tears and impassioned tones showed how much we cared.

We had been discussing family relationships and roles. Different analyses revolved around interpretations of who and what is to blame for the crisis of the family in our day. Where do we point the finger? So things are desperately wrong! Who done it? And how, after we isolate the virus, do we boldly restore wholeness?

Our minds grope for explanations, for accurate analysis, for expert insight. And depending on our perspective, we lay the blame at the feet of the feminists, the traditionalists, or maybe on capitalism or the media or all-American individualism.

We're up against a massive phenomenon that defies simplistic analysis. The security of predictable patterns in the past now looks appealing to us, just as it did to the Israelites, compared to the frightening uncertainty of our modern wilderness. Take us back to Egypt!

Take us back! we cry. Take us back to when Mom stayed home all day and Dad's paycheck buttered the bread. Take us back to when you knew who sat at the head of the table and who must be silent at the table. Take us back to when only men preached the Scriptures and when women prepared the church dinner.

Those were the days . . . Those were the days when each knew where to belong and each knew how to function. There was a wide cultural and even church consensus about family and community life. The rules of the game were clear. And anyone knows that a game where the players can't agree on the rules is no fun to play. A house where the builders can't agree on the design and materials is no fun to build, or to live in.

And so we plead, take us back to recover family life as it used to be, that powerful archetype of the traditional family. It appeals because it worked. (At least we can garner plenty of evidence that makes it appear to have worked, though one could argue that there are as many different kinds of "traditional" families as there are non-traditional.) The glue of marriage stuck. The children knew whom they were to obey. The dinner table was amply spread with homemade delights and all gathered to begin the meal on cue—grace led by Dad.

If it worked so well, why call it a return to Egypt? If it was so good, why liken it to slavery? Perhaps it is Eden that we see in those mythic bygone days of remembered family bliss. Here is where things turned emotional in our family discussion. We tried on a variety of biblical allusions for size and chose one or the other according to our personal fit. Take us back to Egypt! Take us back to Eden!

Where is it we go when we go back? What draws us back? Why

look back at all? How far back must we go to find a helpful reference point?

We have a collective memory as a people. Admittedly, the modern world is managing to savage it, scrambling the cohesiveness of that memory. But even so, one can still find strong residues of memory that connect us with earlier times and stories. When intimidated by today's massive fragmentation, each of us can go scurrying back our memory lanes to tap into the wisdom of days gone by. Will we find wisdom or folly? That is the peril of the search. But we look back nonetheless, and often as not receive some direction for the future.

Were things really better a generation or two ago than they are now? Clearly this is where our memory files prove to be highly selective. What for one looks like the harmony of Eden, to another resembles the rigidity and oppression of Egypt.

We're in the wilderness, regardless of our interpretation of how we arrived here. Whether or not we were doing something right a couple generations ago, the seeds of disintegration and disillusionment were as present then as were the redeeming qualities of family harmony.

When God led the people of Israel out of Egypt, God led them away from the known into the unknown—away from predictable patterns into the unfamiliar. God led them toward a promised land because their current situation had become unbearable. But the transition from being slaves and victims to becoming a free, covenanted, mature people was excruciating. Only the tiniest minority survived the ordeal. And more than once the people pled with Moses to take them back to Egypt. The price of attaining freedom was far higher than any of them had anticipated. And yet, the promised land, flowing with milk and honey, was always there for those who didn't lose heart.

God beckoned them forward into the future, away from the security of the past. God reorganized their life together, strengthened their identity as a people, and called them to be a light to all nations.

There's no going back to Egypt or to Eden, however much our selective memory file may evoke pictures of a more stable, serene era. Our times are shaky, uncertain, frightening and exhilarating all in one. It's the nature of the wilderness, untraveled, unfamiliar, leading nowhere in particular. For those who lose sight of the promised land these times mean certain death. But for those who keep the vision burning, who dare to believe in a future and a hope, the way will become known as we walk in it.

5.
Freedom Gone to Seed

We received a cassette recording of South African freedom songs one Christmas from Gerald's brother. Little did we know what was in store for us.

I distinctly remember the riveting moment when in our own living room, I first played the tape. As the lead song, "O Freedom," rang out, it reached straight to the heart, stirring a deep resonance. All else lapsed into oblivion as the passionate, yearning voices drew me in.

"O freedom, O freedom, O freedom; Freedom is coming, O yes I know!" With the second verse, "O Jesus; Jesus is coming, O yes I know!" their confident hope became even more heartrending.

The longing for freedom and the longing for Jesus went hand in hand. The coming of freedom and the coming of Jesus were seen as one. The simplicity of the song belied the power of the message. Who, when roused by its confidence, wouldn't be inspired to claim their birthright as free children of God? No wonder the freedom songs were banned in South Africa.

As the walls came tumbling down in eastern Europe during the fall and winter of 1989-90, the world gasped with disbelief. Who could have foretold such a massive, swift demise to totalitarian rule? No one in their wildest imaginations! Yet when the emboldened masses laid hold on the freedom that was rightfully theirs, the ironclad monolith of centralized rule crumbled before their eyes. The surge of relief and joy spread around the world. Marxism had been weighed and found wanting. Freedom carried the day!

We are called to freedom. It is our human destiny. From the dawn of time God created us to be free. *"For freedom* Christ has set us free,"
Paul exulted. "Stand firm, therefore, and do not submit again to a yoke of slavery." And with resounding clarity, *"For you were called to freedom,* brothers and sisters . . ." (Galatians 5:1, 13a NRSV, emphasis added).

The freedom to which we're called, Paul implies, is not so much a wild joyride as it is a carefully discerned course between two snare-filled fields. He warns his readers not to submit again to a yoke of slavery. Don't give in to those who would ensnare you in legalisms and leftover litmus tests for purity. Don't imagine that the gates of heaven will open to you because you have restricted yourself to rules of righteousness legislated by government, church or parental authorities. For freedom, Christ has set you free. Those who would legislate an arbitrary morality are forcing a yoke of slavery on you that you must resist.

However, Paul proceeds to warn about the perils in the opposite field of snares. Freedom is no panacea but is fraught with possibilities for abuse. "You were called to freedom; only do not use your freedom as an opportunity for self-indulgence, but through love become slaves to one another." Freedom is not meant to degenerate into rank individualism that puts self's whims and fancies at the fore. Freedom as an escape from all that was enforced by an external disciplinarian must now bear the fruit of an inner discipline that puts love for others at the fore. Curious that the way to avoid both the perils of enforced slavery and the perils of self-indulgence is seen as *voluntary slavery* to one another in love.

The movement to the New World in the 17th-20th centuries, away from religious intolerance, and away from autocratic kings, was a freedom movement. The new American society would be a massive experiment in individual freedom. Emancipation from the rule of a few patriarchs and kings to the rule of the many would be to embrace the freedom that is our destiny.

But the bloom of freedom that created this nation has disintegrated.

Author Donald Joy cites a writer from *The New Yorker* who argues that "if one examines the points of disintegration separately, one finds they have a common cause—the overriding value placed on the idea of individual emancipation and fulfillment, in the light of which the old bonds are seen not as enriching but as confining." And Urie Bronfenbrenner of Cornell University faults "a national neglect of children and those primarily engaged in their care—America's parents. A broken TV set or a broken computer provoke more indignation and more action than a broken family or a broken child" (Joy, 1988, pp. 85-89).

Freedom carries both promise and peril. That which was meant to bloom with an undiminished, lavish beauty in this new world has gone to seed. We have blundered unwittingly from the rule of the fathers into the rule of the selfish ego, having neglected on a massive scale the inner discipline that enables us to hold the high middle ground. The prince of slavery scoffs.

Jesus said, "If the Son sets you free, you shall be free indeed." In truth, only when freedom and Jesus are wed do we know the fullness of liberation.

6.
Free, But O So Fragile

During a summer camping trip we spent days among the scenic sand dunes on the western coast of Lake Huron. It soon became clear that many, many other campers were drawn to its fossil strewn beaches and dunes. On our treks back and forth between campsite and beach there were signs warning us not to walk on the dunes. This beautiful, fragile environment with its unique vegetation was put at tremendous risk by the very people who apparently valued it by showing up to recreate there. They scrambled over it, dragging boats and swimming gear over it, rolling down and digging in it.

Local environmentalists and rangers had painstakingly planted thousands of grass plants to hold the dunes in place under the onslaught. Each individual plant's tenacious hold on the eroding dune served a vital role in preserving the precarious beauty of the place. Rangers requested that people please use the wooden walkways provided to guard against further damage. Sadly, some still disregarded the careful, explicit instructions.

As moderately well-off Americans, we have yet to come to terms with the fragility of our support system—the web of relationships that sustains our well-being. Many of us, coming from relatively stable families and communities, have taken for granted the foundation that structured our formation. We've opted for mobility, for a pursuit of personal happiness. The fragile family ecosystem that nurtured us is threatened with massive disintegration under the onslaught of erosion, and yet we hardly pause a moment to mourn its demise.

I write as a member of a church family that has traditionally been sectarian and ethnic. Along with many of my generation, I imagined that we could throw off the old constrictions of such a community and still survive. More and more we see that the community with stability and security we enjoyed as youngsters, archaic and narrow as it may have seemed, *was* at least a community of reference. It was an ordered, interdependent community that is far from easy to recreate.

What is our legacy for our children?

There is in the air a tremendous unease about the future. In unguarded moments we worry that what we got in exchanging old-fashioned family values for independence and self-expression is perhaps more anarchy than we're equipped to tame.

Arlie Hochschild, sociologist at the University of California, writes in *Newsweek*, "Husbands, wives, children are not getting enough family life. Nobody is. People are hurting." We want it both ways: a tolerant, free and open society, yet also an environment to preserve the value of family life—stable, nurturing, and prepared to sacrifice personal goals (Special Edition, 1990, pp. 17-18).

The pendulum is swinging away from seeing the family as a nest of oppression and pathology (a popular theme for decades), toward acknowledging it as the basic social unit on which the health of a whole society depends.

Public policy experts have rediscovered an institution that can best help America's children: the family. Such is the conclusion of a report entitled "Putting Children First," issued in September 1990 by the Progressive Policy Institute, a think-tank based in Washington, D.C.

This apparently self-evident conclusion comes only after the crisis of the family has reached such proportions that it is no longer possible to delude ourselves that schools and governmental agencies can patch up the problem. These public institutions were only meant to supplement the process of development that should begin at home.

While the evidence mounts that "home sweet home" is anything but sweet for many people, and downright abusive for some, we dare not lose sight of the vision of home life as it is meant to be. To invigorate the vision of life at home that encompasses stable, loving, lifelong relationships is not to deny that home life for many is horrific. It is rather to assert with a full heart of compassion that a proliferation of government bureaucracies is not ultimately the solution to the crisis in our families. Rather, it is a renewed commitment to change things at the heart of our homes, to refocus our energies to empower struggling families, making it possible to live together in peace.

It takes a hardy species of grass to hold on in the hostile environment of a dry, windswept dune. Though the ecosystem as a whole may be fragile under the onslaught of sun and surf lovers, each individual grass plant's roots express a remarkable tenacity. When the determination to preserve life is shared by many others, the dune as a whole, with its precarious and wondrous beauty, may survive.

7.
A Birthright Despised

At the dinner table one evening we read the story of Jacob's stew and Esau's birthright. It wasn't the first time our nine- and twelve-year-old boys had heard the story, but their incredulity at Esau's flippant disregard for his inheritance was undiminished.

"That was so dumb!" they protested. He could have eaten a few crackers, one suggested, and staved off his hunger pangs until he had time to prepare some food.

In hindsight, Esau's behavior does seem mighty "dumb," giving away his right to a secure future, his firstborn advantage over his brother, for the satisfaction of a full belly. The biblical writer tells us that Esau despised his birthright. He must have placed little stock in what he would gain in the long run, preferring the real pleasure available now. Or was it that he had grown so adept at getting what he wanted that, birthright or no, he felt confident he could control the outcome? Whatever his motivation, his impetuous bravado completely disintegrated when he learned that Jacob, who all along had his eye on the long-term implications of events, had received their father's blessing. Hearing this, Esau "cried out with an exceedingly great and bitter cry. 'Have you not reserved a blessing for me?'" he begged his father, and he "lifted up his voice and wept."

The marriage covenant and the intact, bonded family are a birthright, it seems to me, a gift of committed interrelatedness whose structure and significance were bequeathed to us by generations gone by. Even though in some cases people need to be released from destructive marriages, we are largely failing to esteem our birthright. In countless ways we are both hearing and giving the message that wholesome family life and a marriage that endures are rarely worth the effort.

Marriage and family are either an inheritance that we protect and cherish with great effort as one of life's finest treasures, or an inheritance that is disposable; a birthright that can be traded in for the immediate satisfaction of a pot of stew.

And who is it that pays the price for the parents' low esteem for this birthright? U.S. Census Bureau figures report that 1.1 million children have their families broken by divorce each year. What does such a statistic mean for the children involved? asks theologian Elizabeth Achtemeier:

> It means that many children are now the central figure in bitter disputes between their parents over their custody and that some of them are "kidnapped" by the noncustodial parent. It means that the teenagers among them must make the choice of which parent they want to live with—must make that choice when they have no desire to lose either parent. It means that some little ones get shunted back and forth continually between homes and schools, until they no longer know where they live or indeed just who they are. . . . It means that most of those children must now adjust to the fact that their father or mother is dating or living with someone else who will eventually replace the absent parent, that the new marriage often brings with it a bewildering array of stepbrothers and stepsisters but that it too is likely to fail, plunging the child into further trauma, further anger and guilt and confusion (Achtemeier, 1987, p.22).

A January 1991 article in *The Washington Post*, entitled "Therapists Rethink Attitudes on Divorce," quotes a mother on the way to her third divorce saying, "I've always thought that if parents can't bring a child up in a happy home, everyone is better off if there's a divorce."

Until recently, the article continues, psychologists, sociologists, marriage counselors and family scholars wouldn't have argued much with her. In fact, a good deal of elite opinion in the past focused more on "the expansion in *freedom for adults* than on the possible *harm to children* of broken marriages" (emphasis added).

We were naive in thinking that divorce didn't have serious impact on kids, admits Anna Benningfield, president-elect of the American Association for Marriage and Family Therapy. New studies show that the harmful effects of divorce on children are longer lasting than had been thought earlier. Children of divorce perform less well in school, have more behavioral and psychological problems and a greater tendency as adults to divorce than children raised by both biological parents.

Admittedly, domestic violence and other problems of high-conflict marriages are harmful for children, and even experts intent on saving marriages acknowledge that divorce is sometimes the best alternative, the *Post* continues.

But a renewed look at the kind of long-term risk factors that divorce creates for children has produced statistics that are profoundly disturbing.

"For years experts said, 'Once the initial trauma wears off, kids make adjustments.' Well, so do people in prisons and mental institutions," remarks John Guidubaldi, psychology professor at Kent State University and past president of the National Association of School Psychologists. "The pertinent question is: Are those adjustments healthy? The weight of evidence has become overwhelming on the side that they aren't."

Guidubaldi continues, "People simply aren't putting enough effort into saving their marriages. *I think the old argument of staying together for the sake of the kids is still the best argument.*"

One is compelled to ask whether we have so thoroughly sold out our birthright that it is beyond recovery. Can our society survive when more and more of our children watch helplessly while the cradle of their well-being is dismantled for lack of mutual commitment to the family whole?

Donald Joy, author of several books on bonding and sexual integrity, suggests convincingly that divorce is more related to pressures to be sexually active before marriage than to any other single cause. When sexual intimacy is saved for one exclusive relationship, it becomes the glue of a powerful bond. The innocence and wonder of awakening together to the joys of sexuality forge an intimacy that often unites two lovers for life (Joy, 1979, p.42).

Given our social milieu, where sexual permissiveness is encouraged by most of the popular media, and by the majority of U.S. adults (according to Gallup polls), the current fragmentation of families is the bitter fruit of a despised birthright. The children born in a society without a strong commitment to preserve full sexual intimacy for covenanted marital relationships are heirs to an empty pot—a hollow farce of all that was meant to be. As long as the expansion of our own personal freedom as adults takes priority over our commitments to the "least of these," the blessing of coming home to our true inheritance will forever elude us.

8.
Rachel Weeping for Her Children

In the modern scenario of freedom gone to seed, it is the children who are the victims. On an unprecedented scale they are being robbed of their rightful inheritance. And their pain as victims is devastating because it usually happens at home, where intimacy and trust are meant to flourish.

If every divorce, every budgetary decision, every illicit sexual encounter, every career choice, every list of priorities was measured for its effect on a child's well-being, we would as a nation be held liable for massacring the spirit and future of our children. Rachel is weeping for her children and will not be comforted!

Home has become an afterthought, relegated to the fringes of our busy days. Many families make their home a crash pallet, not a place to preserve and cultivate life together; a battleground, not a thriving hub of simple shared pleasures; a launch pad for personal ambitions, not an arena for self-giving nurture. Poor and rich alike (though for differing reasons) have been losing the home as a stable, warm environment where children can grow into healthy adults.

Trouble at home is writ large on a national scale. The 1980s were a "terrible decade for children," reports a February 1991 article in *The Washington Post*. The U.S. saw substantial increases in the percentage of its children in poverty, juveniles who are incarcerated, out-of-wedlock births and violent teen deaths.

The American School Board Journal reports that children now make up 40% of America's poor. A decade ago the poorest segment in our society was the aged; now it is our children.

Other reports indicate alarming increases in depression among adolescents, suicide rates of children, and deaths of children due to abuse and neglect.

It is far from easy to grow up in North America today. The prevalence of these troubles raises important questions about the character of our society, contends Perry London, professor in the Harvard University Graduate School of Education. "When impediments to sane growth are epidemic among the youth of a nation, as is true of American society today," he observes, "the issues that plague the lives of people are more than personal problems. They are not simply signs of the health and welfare of children, but of the character of the society, the quality of the civilization, and, perhaps, the prospects for its future."

When the disease is so widespread, how and where does one effect the cure? Does the answer come in more exhortations to a poor single mother to get her life together, or to the homeless unemployed father to shape up? Is exhortation toward higher moral standards the solution for countless parents who are themselves the victims of dysfunctional homes? Are we not all perhaps victims of a plague so pervasive that none of us can be held personally accountable when family relationships go wrong?

From the protected vantage point of my middle-class comfort, I find it alarmingly easy to cast aspersions on individual victims of true *societal disorders.* My righteous self rises up in anger at every married couple who can't keep it together, at every mother and father who fail to deal responsibly with their commitments. I want to scream at all those who play with sex, who exploit and tantalize youth or who romanticize extra-marital liaisons—*Think of the children!* What you are doing is directly related to the health and well-being of the little ones who are entrusted to your (and our) care. *Grow up!*

We want to hold people personally accountable for their mistakes. And we must! Clean, righteous anger may be precisely what it takes to return some semblance of propriety to personal and national behavior. Yet all the pontificating in the world isn't going to change the behavior of those parents who themselves are crying out for love and healing. Self-righteous lectures are pointless when the "little child" in that so-called "irresponsible adult" is wounded and never had the nurture needed to grow up. How can we hold people accountable for neglecting their children when they themselves never received a parental blessing, when they are shaped by degrading poverty, when their own birthright was nonexistent?

Those of us with abundant education, resources and the luxury to choose from an array of options—it is we who must be held accountable. In fact, to a large extent, we of socially privileged classes are the perpetrators of this epidemic. Because we who have options have often chosen for self-interest ahead of family commitments, it is we who have spread the disease, pretending that we can pamper ourselves without any negative consequences. I think it would be accurate to observe that the more choices we have, the less often we (both women and men) have *chosen for the children.* It also appears that the more possibilities for us to achieve personal and career goals, the more we have come to view children as an obstacle. And the more we feel able to control our own destiny, the less we are willing to deal with the unpredictable distracting dynamo that is a child.

"The latchkey lifestyle you gave us in the name of your own 'freedom,'" writes college senior Daniel Smith-Rowsey in *Newsweek*, "has made us a generation of missing parents and broken homes" (July 1, 1991).

Time and time again we have made lifestyle decisions that put our marriages and our children at a tremendous disadvantage. We have failed to comprehend, as one person put it, the "gift of extravagant grace" that is each child. We have failed to make the sacrifices that would give our children the kind of parenting they need.

Will the cries of our children move us to repent, or are we already deaf to their pleas? The least we can do is to weep with Rachel, and refuse comfort until our children are honored with the tender loving care that is their birthright.

9.
A Saving Memory

"Mama," Greta said to me, "isn't it nice that you have such a good rememberer in your house?"

"I do? Who can remember so well?"

"I can. I can remember when I was born." And with exuberance, "I can even remember when you were born and when Daddy was born." I smiled.

Memory. What a priceless treasure! One that grows more precious with age. This past Sunday, for our Thanksgiving service, we were each to bring a symbol of something for which we are thankful. I took a photo album filled with pictures of our years in Yugoslavia. Now, when all hell has broken loose there, with all manner of vicious atrocities, I cling to the memory of how it was when Serbs and Croats worshipped together and drank sweet black Turkish coffee together in our home. When things go wrong in a marriage, in a church, in a nation, it is the memory of another time and place when all was well that gives me courage—a memory of the way it was meant to be. Perhaps, after all, it is the memory of Eden from which all hope originates.

Over and over again God reminded the people of Israel that when things were desperately wrong it was because they had forgotten who they were, who God is, and that the Law was given to them for their own good. Jeremiah writes, "A cry is heard on the barren heights, the weeping and pleading of the people of Israel, because they have perverted their ways and have forgotten the Lord their God. . . . I am bringing disaster on this people," the Lord said. . . "because they have not listened to my words and have rejected my law" (Jeremiah 3:21, 6:19; NIV).

The news this morning showed the children of Basra, Iraq, walking through open sewage running through their streets because their town's sewage treatment plant had been damaged by American bombs many months before. It showed them anemic and starving without adequate medicine or food. Another news report from Vukovar, in eastern Croatia (Yugoslavia), showed injured babies and others born in basements during the seige, now being hoisted onto an evacuation truck. More footage showed pale, fearful children walking away from their homes down streets strewn with rubble and corpses, clinging to their weeping mothers.

"Oh God," I cried, "save the children. Save them from the madness of their parents and the madness of other parents of other children who have done this to them."

Is this the beginning of the end? One doesn't need to be alarmist to wonder whether the final days are at hand. When the children of the world are neglected and abused in as many different ways and places as they are now, it doesn't take an apocalyptic vision to anticipate that there may be no future worth living.

After one particularly dismal report of the massive, multiple, deadly toxic waste dumps left over from decades of nuclear weapons production, I felt close to despair. It will require billions of dollars for even minimal cleanup, not to mention the insanity it was to make the stockpiles of obscene overkill in the first place—all dollars that represent food taken out of the mouths of starving children.

But it isn't only toxic waste dumps that our children must cope with. They are bombarded every day with reports about ozone depletion, rainforest destruction, senseless violence in the streets, red tides on the beaches, the AIDS epidemic, condoms distributed like candy at the school dining room, acid rain, depictions of violence and sex masquerading as entertainment . . . ad nauseam. How do we instill hope in our children? They look to us all the time to tell them it will be all right.

God spoke through Jeremiah: "Consider then and realize how evil and bitter it is for you when you forsake the Lord your God and have no awe of me. . . . This is the nation that has not obeyed the Lord its God or responded to correction. Truth has perished; it has vanished from their lips" (Jeremiah 2:19, 7:28; NIV).

Where is my little rememberer? I need her to reach back with me for a true memory of beginnings. As I grope in a dark fog of despair, might there be a memory that can, like a lifeline, connect me with timeless truths that stretch across all of human history? "Stand at the crossroads and look," says the Lord, "ask for the ancient paths, ask where the good way is, and walk in it, and you will find rest for your souls. . . . Obey me, and I will be your God and you will be my people. Walk in all the ways I command you, that it may go well with you" (Jeremiah 6:16, 7:23; NIV).

But aren't we desperately outnumbered, those of us who span the centuries with our commitment to the life-giving law of God? Isn't our determination to be faithful despite overwhelming odds ludicrous? Again God speaks through Jeremiah: "If you can find but one person who deals honestly and seeks the truth, I will forgive this city" (Jeremiah 5:1, NIV).

It is for the sake of our children that my memory has been activated. If all our children can see is the present and the ominous future, they will lose hope. But if we can take them back with us, holding onto the interwoven strands of the true memory of God's people, hope will forever spring anew from the Source.

One of our favorite times for remembering is when Grandpa Wenger visits and regales us with Bible stories and with stories from his childhood in the Shenandoah Valley. On a recent visit he told stories that he'd heard as a boy from old "Uncle Pete" Hartman, who had been a young lad here in our very own valley during the Civil War. The stories of young men and families right here in years gone by, refusing to kill their "enemies" because their God had shown a more perfect way, braced our spirits. A lifeline stretched across the generations right into our own living room.

10.
No More Denying It,
We Are Homeless

At a women's retreat last winter, the focus of our discussion was mother-daughter relationships. Many a participant found it profoundly liberating to examine her own relationship to her mother and to come to terms with the power that relationship continues to wield years later. For some the process of differentiating themselves from what was hurtful proved very significant in releasing new visions for relationships with children and others.

There are many facets to the relationships we have with our parents—many subtle aspects that played into forming us. Even with a lifetime of examination we can't plumb the depths. We continually grope for explanations, mining our memories for insights into what made us who we are. What is it about our parents that we want to emulate? What is it that wounded or bound us?

Regardless of how wholesome or harmful we experienced those formative relationships, there is that within each of us that longs to come home to the home that was meant to be—to the home where we are rocked and sheltered. The yearning to come home, to be cherished for who we are, is one of the most universal and profound longings experienced by humankind. Even for persons who rush to escape their own home because it was destructive, the search for the home that should have been never ends. And those who have survived the bitterness and pain of a dysfunctional family often resolve the more firmly to create a thriving home for themselves and their children. Their vision for home as it should be is sharpened.

The ideals of family life have changed much less than the practice of it, write Peter and Brigitte Berger. Even those with less than the ideal continue to uphold the old ideal of parents living together and sharing responsibility for their children and for each other (Berger and Berger, 1983, p.185).

The younger son in Jesus' story of the two sons left home with the impetuousness of a passionate man eager to experience life. In his need to test the limits of personal ambition he chose to repudiate cultural and family expectations. His quest led him, not to a new community or satisfying work, but to lonely despair. In the midst of that despair, he came to his senses, recognizing as if for the first time the goodness of that which he had earlier despised. He needed, somehow, to experience homelessness before he could truly appreciate home, before he could envision a return home and the new basis on which he would function after his return.

Each of our lives is punctuated by comings and goings. We leave home over and over again—physically, emotionally, spiritually. We move out, set up on our own, sometimes in a distant country. But we return. Over and over again we return, in one way or another—perhaps not to a physical house, but to a memory of home that originally defined for us the sum total of life on this earth. Our compasses orient themselves in relation to home, no matter where on the face of the earth we are. And as we establish our own grown-up homes, our compasses swing wildly back and forth between our parental home and our own variation on the theme. Never are we beyond the reach of the magnetism that turns our thoughts toward home. Even if that home remains a longing for what never was, it still exerts a powerful pull toward a place to belong—in family, in community.

If, as we pursue some lonely, private destiny, we are graced with a flash of insight and see our deplorable homelessness for what it is, we may yet come home. If we awaken to the desperate reality that our flagrant neglect of life at home has brought on us, we may yet be able to revive our life-support system.

The tension between individual destiny and family responsibility will always tug us around. There will be times when we need to leave for a far country, need to disengage from the ties that bind too tightly. But when we come to our senses, our desperate homelessness will compel us to try again to build a home that endures. Grace will tug us back to invest in and revitalize those relationships on which our life depends. And for many of us, rekindling life at home will require a new vision of what that life should entail—mutuality and celebration.

Visser t'Hooft writes: "It is time to ask if true emancipation is not that found by the prodigal son when he returned to his father's house—a house where, because of the love which it contained, order was not domination, nor freedom anarchy" (1982, p.xi).

11.
An Everlasting Love

Last night, on our way to bed at midnight, Gerald carried our three-year-old Greta to the toilet one last time and then tucked her back into bed. As he tenderly nestled her head on his shoulder I overheard the now familiar refrain: "I'll love you forever, I'll like you for always. As long as I'm living, my baby you'll be." It comes from a children's book entitled *Love You Forever* by Robert Munsch. We gave it to our children last Christmas and I read it aloud at two extended family reunions where it evoked many tears.

Last night our hearts were heavy with the news of a worsening marital crisis in our extended family. It was an evening for grieving the fragility of relationships—among our church family, between friends and in our own families. Gerald's soft words to his daughter became for me a prayer. "O God, may it be that we'll love each other forever. May it be that as long as we live, the bond of our love will survive every crisis, every burst of anger, every misunderstanding. May it be that love will prove to be stronger than everything else that would pull us apart."

In a world where countless relationships that once vibrated with warmth and laughter now languish because of neglect or outright hostility, a love that endures is the exception. It's one thing to say "I'll love you forever" to a small child cuddling close to your heart in an abandonment of trusting repose. It's quite another to know a love that undergirds through all the confusion, changes and heartbreak of a lifetime.

Change wreaks havoc on once-upon-a-time intimate, safe relationships. Change is inevitable. And the second law of thermodynamics suggests that not only is change inevitable, but change will naturally be in the direction of breakdown, deterioration, coming apart. The enduring quality of unconditional love, a love that rocks another in one's arms, year after changing year with the reassuring words, "I'll love you forever," *is not inevitable.* It is miracle! It is grace!

On Mother's Day this year at church I plan to preach on *Love You Forever.* The story depicts a mother and her growing son. Mothers may come closest, at least in cultural lore, to exemplifying unconditional love. But there is in our spiritual heritage an oft-overlooked quality of "father love" that is exemplified again and again in the one whom Jesus called "Abba": "I have loved you with an everlasting love, I have drawn you with loving kindness. I will build you again, and you will be rebuilt. . . because I am Israel's father" (Jeremiah 31:3, 4a, 9b, NIV). I have loved you with an *everlasting love!*

III.

There Is a Way Home

12.
A Radical Act of Discipleship

I think the time has come for a revolution of priorities at home. Home-based ministry, be it to one's own children, to neighbors, to the elderly, to any who are forgotten and left out, needs to be reinvigorated. What better place than the home for children to see Christ-like ministry modeled day after day? What is more needed in our isolationist neighborhoods than homes that provide a warm circle of tender loving care? What could give a greater influx of energy to the church than a growing (rather than shrinking) core of folks free to volunteer for service to the community?

I grant this is a minefield—an area of discourse so sensitive and fraught with dilemmas that no matter what is said, someone will feel stepped on. But let me assert, as did LaVerna Klippenstein, popular Canadian Mennonite columnist, that two-parent families who choose to live on one full-time salary or a couple of part-time salaries to free up time for presence at home and voluntary service to others are making a radical and essential statement about Christian ministry in our day.

I must at least partially qualify what I am suggesting. I know that not everyone has these options: very often full employment is due to financial or emotional necessity. And surely not every home is made better by having a full-time parent. Many persons (mostly women) who have devoted full time to the home have become disillusioned and bitter. Nor is it always the case that if both parents are employed full-time there is no family life or community service. And many single parents manage to hold job and family together with astounding tenacity. Nevertheless, there is good reason to examine further what is at stake in the nurturing of life at home.

An article in the *Chicago Tribune* some years back featured the world's "smartest person"—a woman with an IQ of 230, so smart she could chop her IQ in half and still be above average. One remark she made in the interview: "I can't imagine just staying home and doing nothing but taking care of someone. Anybody can take care of a baby." This woman also called marriage "stultifying" and said there are too many kids in the world for her to contribute any more. Clearly the implication to be drawn from these comments is that if you have brains it is beneath your dignity to care for children, and if you stay home to take care of someone, you are doing nothing of value and don't need brains for it.

A friend who visited us, whose husband was working on a doctorate at an Ivy League school, remarked that in their university community, if you admit you are a homemaker, "you count for zero."

I'm reminded, too, of a seminary professor who lamented the injustice perpetrated in families because many wives have been obligated to "forego personal development" in order to care for the family, thus freeing husbands to pursue personal growth.

Where did we get this twisted notion that to stay home with children is to stagnate? Who fabricated the fiction that to make a home counts for nothing? Is it barking into the wind to proclaim that homemaking for the sake of one's children and neighborhood is worthy of a woman's *and* a man's best efforts; that parenting stimulates unparalleled growth in the parents as well?

The time has come to revive the arts of homemaking and rekindle the hearth; to recapture the trembling wonder of a child that shatters one's complacency; to allow ourselves to be humbled by the daily tasks of child care; and consciously to create a rhythm of meaningful activity, a place of devotion, a house of peace. But we must revive the homemaking arts on a new footing.

Reclaiming the home turf means resolving to reintegrate men's and women's work and to interweave home and work into a harmonious pattern. Homemaking means to build community with children and neighbors and to establish worship and celebrative rituals that actively shape family traditions.

Children are not liabilities or a drain on personal growth. Nor is home a backwater of ill repute. In our self-indulgent generation, children are a primary source of conversion. Transforming our isolated, privatized dwellings into home-based communities where life and worship are nurtured is a sacred calling.

Now is not the time for airy-headed romanticism that pines for the olden days of little houses on the prairie. Rather, it is time for hardheaded realism and gutsy determination to make job decisions and personal sacrifices for the common good—the good of our children, ourselves and our society.

13.
Turning Our Hearts to the Children

The other day my father described a local ministerial gathering addressed by the police chief of Manheim Township, in southeast Pennsylvania. The chief spoke of a significant increase in the volume of crime his force deals with in their apparently quiet suburban neighborhoods. He anticipated a dramatic rise in delinquency during the next decade.

Lamenting the trends, he wished we could "just get the parents to stay at home with their children—spend time with them." The family is so fragmented—one parent goes here, one there; they drop one child off here, another there, and give money to a third and send him off to be with peers.

Many parents have bought into the concept of "quality time" with their children, supposing that short but intensely good spurts of interaction with their children will compensate for all their absences. Quality time, says George Barna, a leading researcher of family and societal trends, is *one big myth!* Quantity of time together is absolutely critical in giving our children the parenting they need to develop into healthy adults. There is no substitute for structuring our life so as to often *be with* our children.

As Urie Bronfenbrenner observes,

The young cannot pull themselves up by their own boot-straps. It is primarily through observation, playing, and working with others older and younger than themselves that children discover both what they can do and who they can become, that they develop both their ability and their identity. . . Hence to relegate children to a world of their own is to deprive them of their humanity and ourselves as well.

Yet that is what is happening in America today. We are experiencing a breakdown in the process of making human beings human (Joy, 1988, pp. 49, 87).

But there are some hopeful signs in our generation, writes Donald Joy in *Parents, Kids and Sexual Integrity.* Many fathers, disillusioned with depersonalized life on the job, are gravitating toward parental involvement, being present at the birth of their children and more actively participating in their care. The trend has such proportions, he claims, that for the first time, solid research evidence indicates that many junior high children rate their parents as their best friends and best source of knowledge (Joy, 1988, pp. 84-85).

Are we too busy to make our homes thriving hubs of communal fellowship and witness?

The prophecy to Zechariah about his soon-to-be-born son, John the Baptist, was that "he will turn many of the people of Israel to the Lord their God. With the spirit and power of Elijah he will go before him, to *turn the hearts of parents to their children,* and the disobedient to the wisdom of the righteous, to make ready a people prepared for the Lord" (Luke 1:16,17 NRSV; emphasis added).

"Turning the hearts of parents to their children" is portrayed as a *central feature of repentance.* This insight *explodes* with relevance in our generation. The fruit of a truly repentant heart is a softening of that heart toward one's own children; a renewed commitment to devote oneself to the young ones in our charge. To repent of one's sins is in every sense of the word, to come home—to create a place of safety—where life with our children is a daily exercise in discipline and devotion.

And why go home? To care for our children, yes. But also to transform our dwellings into home-based communities where our life together includes and ministers to others. There is a crying need for healthy families and thriving homes to be a source of hope in our neighborhoods. Our homes can be significant mission outposts, places of healing for all kinds of individuals.

During most of our years in what used to be called Yugoslavia, we lived in households with a variety of Yugoslav single friends and families who shared adjoining apartments or a room within ours. In that context we saw time and again the powerful witness it was to the members of our household and to their friends, relatives, and guests as well, to see the way a Christian family lives together—to see a husband and wife relate respectfully; to see a father's attentiveness to his children; to see the way we discipline, attempting to communicate love and limits consistently .

Are we a showcase, ideal family? By no means! But we learned it was instructive to many who watched us managing to live together and usually enjoying the process.

And when our guests happened to join us for our weekly Sabbath meal, breakfast songs, or reading and playing games together, they were able to *see* the Gospel, not by being preached at, but by being included in its outworking of family life together. Worship experiences, when a natural and genuine part of family life, are an inclusive form of evangelism. They don't put guests on the spot. Visitors are simply drawn into the spirit of the event as they sit with us around the table.

Repentance! A turning of hearts to our children. A turning of our hearts toward home where, day after day, the fruits of the Spirit ripen and flourish right where they are most needed.

14.
The Sins
of the Fathers and Mothers

It is a rare conversation among parents of teens that doesn't include a lament about the negative pressures of the youth culture. Parents of today are up against youth peer strength of such enormity that they may be tempted to believe they are irrelevant. We parents resent being mistreated, disregarded without respect.

And yet the values our youth have adopted are those we have given them. Rather than teaching our children to be responsible, we've taught them to prize their youth—because we've clung so tenaciously to our own youthful fantasies. As Kenneth Woodward states so succinctly in a 1990 Special Edition of *Newsweek* on the family, "What the young see enshrined in the media and malls of America are, after all, the values adults put there: consumerism, narcissism and the instant gratification of desire."

Thousands of years ago God painted the picture in even more vivid strokes: "You shall not make for yourself an idol, whether in the form of anything that is in heaven above, or that is on the earth beneath, or that is in the water under the earth. You shall not bow down to them or worship them; for I the Lord your God am a jealous God, *punishing children for the iniquity of parents, to the third and the fourth generation of those who reject me . . ."* (Exodus 20:4,5 NRSV; emphasis added).

In a sharp reversal of historic trends, American youth on their way to the twenty-first century are taking longer to grow up, with much less commitment of any kind, reports Woodward. Experts on the family claim never to have seen anything like it. The period of adolescent self-absorption extends right on into adulthood. Adult qualities of competence, commitment, self-discipline and taking care of others are put on hold. By these standards, Woodward contends, young Americans entering the next century are *far less mature* than were their ancestors at the beginning of the twentieth century.

When it comes to marriage, Woodward continues, young people have grown accustomed to keeping their options open. They sense that marriage requires compromise, negotiation and discipline, habits the youth culture does not emulate. They are reluctant to limit their freedom.

Like love, work has also become for many just one more opportunity for immediate gratification, Woodward finds. American sociologists warned in the 1970s that youth were becoming expert consumers long before they were learning how to produce. Teen earnings are usually spent immediately on cars, clothing, sound systems and other "artifacts of the adolescent good life."

How does one account for this widespread reluctance to grow up? Students in the 1980s are the first generation to have lived their entire lives with the presence of television. Psychologist David Klimek asserts that endless hours of watching TV and listening to radio have bred a "passive population" of youth. It is the ability to grow from *passive consumer* to *active participant* that represents a major passage from childhood to adulthood.

In addition to TV, perhaps the single most significant factor in the youth culture's disinterest in growing up has been the lack of parental support for doing so. "The irony is that we have the best group of educated parents in history doing the least for their own kids," claims historian Maris Vinovskis.

When our children are abandoned, left to cope on their own during the confusing and stress-filled years of adolescence, out of necessity they turn to each other. The peer group becomes the most powerful socializing force. There is a fundamental and disturbing fact, writes Urie Bronfenbrenner—children need adults in order to become human. And he concludes, "What is needed is a change in our patterns of living which will once again bring people back into the lives of children and children back into the lives of adults" (cited in Joy, 1988, p. 87).

There are growing indications that the American dream may have peaked in our generation. Our children and their children will preside over its accelerating demise. We have pushed the instant gratification of our selfishness to its extreme and in so doing depleted the inheritance left for our children. "Don't say you didn't start the fire of selfishness and indulgence," writes college senior Daniel Smith-Rowsey (*Newsweek*, July 1, 1991), "building it up until every need or desire was immediately appeased. Cable TV, BMWs, cellular phones, the whole mall culture has reduced us all to 12-year-olds who want everything *now*."

In his heartrending appeal to parents, that if "any part of you still loves us enough to help us, we could really use it," he says "all we've been left with are the erotic fantasies, aggressive tendencies and evanescent funds of youth. Pretty soon we won't have youth or money, and that's when we may get a little angry."

The sins of the parents—"those who reject me"—are a legacy of punishment for the children for generations to come. We can't say that we haven't been warned.

15.
Let's Get Real

Opinions about what should happen at home are legion. One young mother commented, "I sometimes wish I had lived 100 years ago when everything wasn't a choice. Then I could have been a traditional mother, spent my days with my kids, and just delighted in them without all this ambivalence about career and identity."

Whether this woman's concept of the reality our foremothers experienced is accurate or not, she put her finger on one of the chief dilemmas contemporary women face: there is now no widespread cultural consensus about who we are as women, wives and mothers, and what we are supposed to do.

Rare is the woman today who can say, as a woman of my mother's generation said, "I felt no other calling than to get married and to have children." We are called in our generation to a new dimension of freedom and maturity. To a greater degree we must take responsibility for who we become and how we will serve amid an ever-expanding array of options.

Waves of ambivalence swamp the attempts many of us make to be all things to all people. We sometimes regard women who have made different choices than our own with jealousy or suspicion. Many of us harbor an inordinate amount of guilt for failing ourselves, our husbands, our parents or our children. With heightened expectations about what all we can become, and also more knowledge about what makes for healthy children, we frequently incriminate ourselves for falling short on one front or another.

Yet despite the painful self-doubts which inevitably accompany times of intense growth, and despite the accusations and jealousies, we are blessed in our day with an enormous flowering of women's gifts. We've discovered on a large scale that women, like men, are good at more things than the traditional roles led us to believe. The sense of empowerment has thrust us into the work force in ever-increasing numbers, often to lay claim to careers, salaries and ministries beyond the wildest dreams of our mothers. The freedom to come into our own in many arenas has expanded immeasurably.

Yet even while we thrilled to the new challenges and worked to become "all we were meant to be," we grossly underestimated the tremendous cost our glorification of work would exact from the family whole. The nagging question of what happens to the children in the transition has only belatedly come into view.

The number of mothers in the paid labor force was at 66.7 % in 1990, the highest figure ever recorded by the Bureau of Labor Statistics. The result, writes Paul Taylor in *The Washington Post* (May 1991), is a "family-time famine." Ironically, as the number of mothers entering the labor force has grown, so has their desire to stay home with their children. Many mothers, reports the *Post,* say they would choose to work regardless of family financial needs. But a majority of women *now* say they would consider giving up their jobs if money were not a factor. (Men were not asked the question.) A majority of women and men now say that preschool children get shortchanged when their mothers work outside the home. Both findings, reports Taylor, represent a sharp change from social attitudes that prevailed as recently as two years ago!

"If these numbers aren't a cry of pain, I don't know what is," said Susan Hayword of the polling firm that conducted some of the research mentioned above. "Women seem to have come to the conclusion that they're never going to have it all, and they might die trying. Their attitude is, 'Let's get real, here.'"

Citing an article in *Fortune* magazine, the *Post* observes that in the 1980s work was highly idealized, much as the family was idealized in the 1950s. But now in the 1990s, work is losing its romanticized aura. The bubble has burst. "More people are seeing the wisdom of what their grandmothers would say: work isn't everything; families are important; and there's a very real conflict between the two," quotes the *Post* writer. This trend is being dubbed "the new familism."

I strongly suspect that we have lost a great deal of our humanity and freedom as we have come to regard the "male" work role as the normative human activity. One must seriously question whether women are liberated simply by being enabled to function like men in the public realm.

Leading feminist theologian Rosemary Radford Ruether contends in her book *Sexism and Godtalk* that feminism needs to ask whether instead of our making the male sphere the norm and attempting to assimilate women into it, we should rather move in the opposite direction. "Should we not take the creation and sustaining of human life as the center," she asks, "and reintegrate alienated maleness into it?"

Clearly, women are not automatically redeemed by being incorporated into male political power and business, Ruether writes; nor will men be automatically redeemed by learning to nurture infants and keep house. Some have idealized the home, overlooking the violence so often present there. And yet there are clues to a better humanity in the virtues often associated with women and home in Western society if those virtues are not locked within an exclusive female sphere.

If the new familism brings a revival of commitment to life at home, it heralds a way out of our current wilderness. Feminism has too often uncritically elevated the American dream, contending that women have waited too long, and now it should be their turn "to have it all." Coming to terms with the fact that we can't have it all may bring a semblance of sanity and simplicity amid the fatigue of frenzied ambition. While opinions about what should happen at home may be legion, what can and often does happen at home, when we cherish and celebrate it, is the best that life can offer!

16.
Seeking the Kingdom First at Home

The redistribution of the world's wealth cannot be central,
the concern for ecology cannot be central,
the desire to get out of the rat race cannot be central,
the desire for simplicity itself cannot be central. . . .
Only one thing is to be central: the Kingdom of God.
(Foster, 1971, p. 105)

"What does it mean for me to put God's kingdom first in my family?" asks a seminarian mother.

She continues, "A whole host of feelings and issues surfaces when I think of how living in simplicity affects my family. I have certainly learned something about living with the *opposite* approach this year! For example, my son developed a strep throat last weekend. Two weeks from the end of the seminary term, my first thought was, 'Oh no, I don't have time for this!'

"I haven't had time for a whole lot of things my family has needed or wanted. The children have had to sometimes come home and let themselves into an empty house, stay by themselves while I was off doing something else, or be put off and told to go to another room because I needed to read.

"In spite of all my feelings and beliefs about equal rights and responsibilities in marriage, it just has not always worked for one of us as parents to be available to the children. And it seems to me that when the buck gets passed back and forth, it sometimes stops no-where. The losers are the people we care about most. It just doesn't seem that God's idea of kingdom life in families means parents who are so busy they don't take time to listen, or people who are on edge with each other because they aren't sure who to count on."

Like many other women of my generation, I have often been inspired by Luke's story of Jesus' encounter with Mary and Martha when Jesus commended Mary for sitting at his feet to listen. "Martha, Martha," the Lord answered, "you are worried and upset about many things, but only one thing is needed. Mary has chosen what is better, and it will not be taken away from her" (Luke 10: 41-42, NIV). I imagined that by going to seminary I was becoming more like Mary, meriting Jesus' commendation for choosing what is better.

A woman in my home church confessed through her tears, in the open sharing time of the service, that she so wants to be like Mary, just sitting at Jesus' feet, but the never-ending, urgent household and hospitality chores preoccupy her time. If guests are invited, food must be prepared, the toilet must be cleaned. What does one do to mesh real-life demands with sitting at Jesus' feet?

A wise single mother and grandmother responded. I think we are all Mary *and* Martha, she said. There is no reason you can't sit at Jesus' feet while cooking a meal or while cleaning the toilet. The key is *remembering*—remembering that you are free to pray, listen and wor-ship anytime, anywhere.

One can hope that the dilemma described by the seminary mother is felt with as much intensity by the father, and that the process for discerning how to care for the home front is one of mutual negotiation. It has become clear, however, that, overall, the flow of women into work and study settings outside the home has not been matched by men returning home, causing an enormous deficit in parental nurture at home.

It seems to me that the more apparent it becomes that women are equal and gifted partners with men in all walks of life, and the more readily men demonstrate that homemaking is worthy of a woman's and a man's active commitment—mature individuals will freely choose to stay home for a season.

The true test of our liberation will be our ability to serve the least among us, without expecting much in return. Seeking the Kingdom first will surely mean, in part, structuring our lives so that our children can receive the blessing that is their birthright.

17.
The Family and the Family of God

Lancaster County, Pennsylvania, the heartland for many Mennonites in the eastern United States, became my adopted home in 1966 when my folks retired from mission work in Ethiopia. I lived there for only six of my childhood years before embarking for college and beyond. I have always harbored a profound ambivalence about how much I want to, or even *can* belong to that particular geographical- and faith-community.

We used to kid, as young college radicals, that Lancaster County was a fine place to be *from*, but we would never dream of going back there to live. In fact, when I was first getting acquainted with the man who is now my husband, it was a distinct mark in his disfavor even to be *from there*. I wondered, "Can anything good come from provincial, backwater Manheim (his hometown, near Lancaster)?" To which he would roguishly retort, "Can anything good come from Nazareth?" (I was born in Nazareth, Ethiopia.)

For some of us, it takes a long time to see the beauty and good that is right in front of our eyes. We'd rather go look for it in some far corner of the earth. And many of us need to go away before we can obtain any objectivity about what was good, bad or indifferent in the mix of our formative beginnings.

Little did I know that growing up in Africa, an ocean away from cousins and grandparents, would mean forfeiting meaningful extended family relationships. Not that I was ever given the choice. I simply didn't know it could be otherwise. Perhaps if we had lived closer, the relationships wouldn't have been all that significant either. I don't know. In any event, the church family became for me a more significant extended family than my relatives have been.

My husband's situation was considerably different. After our marriage it gradually dawned on me that Gerald thrived on his extended family relationships. Rather than simply wanting to put them behind him, differentiating himself from his humble, rural beginnings, he continued to cherish people and places that had nourished him. In contrast to me, he had grown up with his cousins, worked in the potato fields together, gone to parochial school and pulled pranks on the teachers together. His uncles and aunts, many of whom had not gone to college, were farmers, hometown pillars, faithful church supporters. Some of them had not moved more than a few miles from their place of birth. They were people who could be counted on year after year—through fires and floods, births and deaths, lean and fat years—stable and reliable.

As time passed and I watched both of the extended families represented by Gerald's parents grow and yet remain resilient, my prejudice evaporated. They had become for me also a towering source of strength—two unpretentious families, with the normal share of faults, but with the tenacity and mutual care to flourish over the long haul. I had blundered, in spite of myself, onto a vein of precious ore. I had married into a rich family legacy of faith and mutual commitment that stands the test of time.

I have experienced fragile community in many different forms, in many places. The promise that if we leave all and seek God's kingdom first, that then houses, brothers, sisters, fathers, mothers, children and fields will be provided, has proven abundantly true—for me in Ethiopia, in Pennsylvania, in California, in Yugoslavia, in Germany, in Illinois, in Virginia. But there is nothing quite so deeply satisfying as the solidarity of a family united across the generations and miles by a common faith and history. I want my children to know the vibrancy of a contemporary faith community, but also, God willing, to know the richness and security of an extended family of relationships where faith and blood run thickly together.

The rampant individualism of our day mocks any legacy of stable community and a family network of mutual care. Individual freedom produces more immediate and tangible rewards, perhaps, but they ring hollow if not related to a family or community of reference—or both, intertwined. There is nothing to compare with the rewards of lifelong commitment. Nothing!

Each family unit is a microcosm of the whole extended family of Christ, writes William Spencer in *Beyond the Curse*. If we take our family responsibility seriously, we must make our home, our spouses, our children, our extended family, and ourselves, the earthly priority for our concerns and actions. Ministry should flow out from our relationships— flowing out of the family whole. How can we presume to share the good things of God with others unless these flow with integrity out of what we are together *already* experiencing in our most intimate relationships? Our words and deeds may then attract others to follow our example of "relational triumph," Spencer concludes, if they can see the fruits of the gospel lived out in three dimensions and full color (Spencer, 1985, pp. 175-177). That is the way it should be: healthy families forming the core of a ministering community. But what recourse is there when the family malfunctions?

The marriage covenant is a conscious decision made by two consenting adults. There is no comparable family covenant, inasmuch as each child had no choice in the matter. And yet, as children, whether we like it or not, by virtue of common parentage we are bound together for better or for worse—if not physically, certainly emotionally. Like it or not, we are made of the same stuff that has gone into forming our family for generations. Whether we wrestle or dance together, whether we choose to stay in relationship or leave, our families simply *are*. They do not go away. They are the enduring reference point from which we must work out our own personhood, our own healing, our own future.

It is the marvel of the *family of God* that it can provide an alternative reference community to the *given* that is one's birth home. And it is that alternative place of shelter that is being called on more and more often to become a healing community. Within the nurture and loving care of that adopted family, individuals may find the wholeness and energy they need to work at the restoration of family relationships.

I recall a comment made by the counselor of a woman in our church community some years ago. This 50-year-old sister in the faith had been severely abused as a child. The church community ministered to her year after year. At times her progress seemed painfully slow. Yet when it came time for her daughter, a beautiful, healthy young woman, to be married, the counselor remarked that the church, because of its enduring commitment to the abused woman's own family, had overcome the negative consequences of the parental abuse within a single generation. Otherwise, the consequences could have carried over into several future generations.

Family reunions—the worst and the best of times, depending on whether or not we have come to terms with our formative family reality. We are bound together for better or worse, even across the generations. May God help us find the healing we need so those "ties that bind" are not chains but an enduring, secure home, a precious legacy for our children. May God enable the church family to become a more determined healing community, committed to restoring mothers and fathers, children and grandparents, spouses and in-laws to one another, so that faith and family are indestructibly intertwined.

18.
Become as Children

An article I recently scanned caught me in a bad moment. The topic was on ways and means to resist the seductions of materialism. One of the means chosen by the author and her husband was not to have children, since one is often tempted to do or buy for the children's sake. To do without children, TV, full-time jobs and to live in the country were all decisions made, the author implied, to enhance their connectedness with God. Materialism, she stressed, produces fragmentation and alienation from ourselves and nature.

While my mind understood the author's rationale, my heart rebelled. What is the good news for those of us who have chosen to have children, to be disciplined about TV, to give ourselves to full-time service in a variety of demanding jobs, and to live in the city? Have we been seduced? Are we disconnected? To be honest, I have sometimes wondered in the hectic flurry of everyday life whether God isn't really saying, "Get thee to a nunnery." Life *could* be so simple!

In a better frame of mind I affirm different lifestyle choices that reflect a variety of personal gifts and callings. But I would argue that it is the very material nature of my children's bodies and needs that has contributed significantly to my connectedness to God. God has come to me over and over again through my children, blessing me, humbling me, connecting me to the good earth, launching me to the heavenlies. To choose not to have children so as to resist materialism sounds to my ears like a blatant contradiction!

My children from their first suckling at the breast to their insightful questions have brought me home to God. Even their requests for Nike shoes and Gameboys and the like provide multiple dynamic opportunities to live out the way of God in our world—wrestling, arguing, praying, retracting and trying again to find the way. Rather than sticking in a narrow rut of what comprises a peace-and-justice simple lifestyle, we are compelled as a family to actively reinterpret what it means every day, interacting with all the stuff, good and bad, that presents itself. And we don't always get it right. But it would be arrogant to imagine we could, if we just avoided all the dilemmas.

A ritual that gives me courage at the end of a day, when my failures as a parent seem most vivid, is to go to the bedside of each child and pray for them one by one as they sleep. It is an acknowledgment for me that no matter how much we do as parents to care for our children, to provide for and discipline them, we are utterly dependent on the grace of God to see us through.

It is humbling to have children. I am reminded every day that life is out of my control. On my own I rather believed the illusion that my life could be controlled, but having children exploded that myth to smithereens. Opening myself to live with children was to make myself vulnerable to pain and unpredictability on a grandiose scale. It has forced me to my knees—to a connectedness that nurtures a profound intimacy with God. To be a parent causes me to crawl much more often onto the lap of my Parent; to become, if you will, as a little child.

IV.

Men and Women and the Return to Eden

19.
The Game is Over

One day Timothy, age nine, noticed the day's mail lying on the table and pointed at one letter addressed to Mr. and Mrs. Gerald Shenk. "That's not fair!" he protested. "Why do they say it that way?"

I couldn't remember elaborating recently on my feelings about titles and addresses, so it was gratifying to see him keying in on a small but significant sore point.

A cousin and his wife lived with us for some weeks this year. They were recently married and our cousin-in-law had opted to retain her maiden name beside her husband's. A cousin of hers, who wrote frequently, stubbornly addressed her letters to "Mr. and Mrs. Doug Shenk," even after "Mrs. Shenk" asked to be addressed with her own name. The cousin in question seemed to be, in her own crusading way, deliberately parading her allegiance to convention.

Oh, the games people play—maneuvers and subtle innuendoes— that keep one from looking at the fundamental question of one's own identity as male or female: interdependent, but also separate and absolutely unique.

In very broad strokes, I see two overreactions to this generation's women's liberation movement. One is to revert to rigid "traditional" roles with the passion of a crusader, as symbolized by this correspondence between two cousins. Fear propels such an overreaction. Men and women are expected to continue playing a role, because that's the way it's supposed to be, whether or not it fits. Rather than freely dancing to the inner rhythm of partners who learn new steps to-gether—flowing in harmony with each other—the dance steps are dictated by "rules for playing the role game properly." There is little sympathy for those who choose to do it another way.

The other overreaction is a more subtle one and relates more directly to men. "Women's lib" has been depicted as energizing and joyful for women, while for men it has often meant the addition of responsibilities, writes Herb Goldberg in his book, *The New Male.* While it may be liberation for women, it is accommodation for men. Again there is fear, but this time, out of fear that he will displease his wife or friend, a man will accommodate to the point where he sells himself short and no longer knows what he wants (Goldberg, 1979, p. 213).

The man is in an impossible bind, writes Goldberg. The woman complains about his domination, his preoccupation with success and his sexist behaviors. Many of the behaviors she castigates him for, however, were the same ones he thought had originally attracted her to him. If he changes to please her, he'll seem to be weak and she'll be repulsed. But if he refuses to change, he's a chauvinist.

The game has turned sour! The rigid role game, "watch how well I can play the part," is no fun anymore. Nor is the "see how well I can play the part *you* want me to play."

What *is* delightful is to celebrate our maleness and femaleness, our common but differentiated humanness. The more at-home I am with myself, secure in my own identity, the more I can respectfully free my partner to be wholly himself.

With fathers moving off the farm into factories, sons lost out on their ability to identify who they were, asserts poet Robert Bly. A boy needs a male model to initiate him into adulthood, to bless him so that he can live truly from the center of his being. Fathers have too frequently been not only absent, but punitive and emotionally with-holding. They've generated legions of sons who felt they never did anything right; sons who were told over and over not to be weak, passive, emotional, feminine, dependent. "Be a man," they were told on the battlefield, on the operating table, in the barroom, and in love making, writes Goldberg (p. 18). And those sons turn right around and tell their sons, "Be a man." One of those young sons quipped on the TV news yesterday, "Now that I've got a gun, I *feel* like a man."

The game is over! At least that must be our prophetic witness, even as we watch it still being pitifully played all around us. Macho roles are not as much fun as guys were led to believe. Being *human*, reentering a world of playfulness, with genuine tears, lifelong intimacy and trust is unsurpassed fun.

Fathers and male adult models in touch with their own humanity can usher in a new generation of sons: sons who are secure in their male self-identity, sons who no longer need to do heroics to be worthy, sons who can act justly, love mercy and walk humbly with God. These sons will be emboldened, with the blessing of their fathers, to step out confidently and embrace a wife as a fully equal partner.

There is a lightheartedness that accompanies such a recovery of self. One can play the role of father and husband and not be played by the role. One can be a mother and wife, loving it, because by mutual agreement the role has been shaped to fit her in the dynamic duo of a free-flowing union.

It is not only in our homes where role games are played out. In our generation we have seen both overreactions illustrated in the character of our church leaders—rigid hierarchy, on one hand, and nice-guy accommodation, on the other. The leaders of today, trying to make up for the heavy-handedness of the past, often appear intimidated and weak, eager not to give offense. Rightly concerned not to exercise power in an autocratic fashion, they are vulnerable to becoming hostages to the wounds of the past. This game too must come to an end.

The other day Gerald came rushing in from his woodpile, red-cheeked from the cold. "Sara," he said, "I've just had an insight! Until our male church leaders have competent and articulate women to work right beside them, they will continue to cower at the rage of women, accommodating anyone out there who thinks males can be blamed for all current ills. Leaders must be free to exercise appropriate authority in a given situation. We need bold, decisive leaders. But let it be men and women *together*, as God intended—co-heirs, co-stewards, rightly discerning the word and will of God."

Now that's a game worth playing!

20.
A *Real* Girl

Last evening the children and I were invited over to our neighbors for hot homemade bran muffins and vegetable soup. Gerald was out of town. During the course of the meal Tara, a vivacious, opinionated nine-year-old asked her mother, "Mom, am I a tomboy?"

"Well, I don't know. What do you think?" her mother responded.

I asked, "Did someone call you a tomboy?"

"No. I read in a book about a girl who got called that and she seemed a lot like me."

"I used to be called a tomboy a lot," her mother said, "because I didn't try very hard to be ladylike, I guess. But I don't like the word. It seems to say that if you are active and adventuresome you're more like a boy than a girl."

"Maybe you're just a *real* girl," I suggested. "You're not giddy or prissy."

"No way!" Tara laughed.

"Yes," her mother agreed. "You are a *real* girl."

The women's movement of the past several decades set off tremors in all sectors of society. Some of the energy and rage it unleashed has been justified and helpful. Some has been misdirected and counter-productive. In its insistence that women function as real people rather than as mere feminine stereotypes, it is absolutely right.

The reason women were drawn to Jesus was that he treated them as real people. In segregated first-century culture, with his genuine respect and affection, Jesus restored woman after woman to her real self. Throughout the stories of Jesus' relationships to women, a song of liberation reverberates. Here was one who not only restored women to personal wholeness but also empowered them to be new persons in dance step with the Spirit of God. Shattering stereotypes, he restored women to their rightful inheritance as daughters of God. He introduced a dizzyingly wonderful new reality: women as they were meant to be, whole, vigorous, bold and filled with joy.

But the heady potion of liberation in our day has sometimes meant that women become so obsessed with their own rights that they ignore the rights of their husbands and children. When women in the first flush of freedom abandon unfulfilling marriages or neglect their children, it looks like strong marriages and family life are somehow in conflict with full equality for women. Are strong families and women's equality incompatible?

The answers to that question go in many directions. If I could venture one, it would be to point us back to Jesus, of whom it was said, "Your attitude should be the same as that of Christ Jesus: Who, being in very nature God, did not consider equality with God something to be grasped, but made himself nothing, taking the very nature of a servant. . ." (Philippians 2: 5-7 NIV).

Jesus, who had equality with God, gave it up. But a person can't give up something until she has it. She can't give up equality until she has experienced what it means to be a full-fledged partner.

When women are denied power over their own lives, they must assert themselves. Women who have been disinherited are justified in laying hold of their rightful inheritance. And then when they come to know themselves as beloved daughters of God and sisters in Christ, they are compelled, as was Christ, as are men, to become obedient even unto death. But until a woman knows who she is, the word to her is, "Pick up your pallet and walk." And if you can't do that, then may God send you friends who will pick it up for you and carry you to Jesus.

Full equality for women and strong thriving families are not incompatible. A woman who knows who she is, and whose she is, can freely use the gifts God has given her to care for her family—even sacrificially. A freely chosen relinquishment of her own rights, poured out in loving service to others can become for her an act of ministry. When a woman is at home with herself and with God, she becomes a powerful force for good in the lives of those around her. As an adventuresome *real* woman, there is no sacrifice too great for her to make so that those whom she serves find wholeness and liberation along with her.

21.
Back to Eden

Numerous comments, both public and private, suggest that if we would just adhere once again to a God-ordained family order, much of what has gone awry in family life would fall quickly back into place. The assumption is that a recovery of the proper order would instantly right something that's gone terribly wrong with family life. What, I wonder, is this "God-ordained" order?

In my experience, "order" terminology is used as shorthand for the vertical, hierarchical view of God over husband over wife over children over dog. The husband is authorized to be the spiritual "head" of the home and of his wife. Her primary responsibility is to submit to his "headship," which in everyday lingo means that he gets his way and she is supposed to give in.

Such a view of "proper order" has done incalculable damage to family relationships. It is "to canonize the fall," writes Donald Joy in *Bonding.* Male-female relationships often begin with an innocent sense of mutual respect and joint partnership. But when they are bent into conformity to this traditional "Christian" hierarchical order, a marked deformity regularly occurs: the woman is taught to serve her husband unquestioningly, losing her own vital connection to God, while the man regards his wife as another part of the world he must control to achieve his own ends (Joy, 1979, p. 26).

When do these "order advocates" acknowledge that in Jesus whose kingdom is upside-down, patterns that permitted males to lord it over females simply because of gender are now absolutely overturned? How tragic to determine the patterns of marriage according to a curse placed on Adam and Eve after they disobeyed God, rather than on what it means to be new creatures in Christ!

Any discussion of marriage that attempts to take seriously the biblical witness must look at the meaning of "headship" and "submission" in the New Testament. Since headship has traditionally implied control and decision-making, while submission has meant a passive falling-in-line, any use of the words is extremely suspect.

What do we do with the biblical material? Do we reject any concept of headship altogether? Is there any mystery to male-female roles in marriage that is lost if we simply see roles as entirely interchangeable?

Paul's instructions to husbands and wives in Ephesians 5: 21-33 in an ingenious way preserves the traditional view of a husband as head, writes theologian Elizabeth Achtemeier, but what is *meant* by headship is radically transformed. There is no "lording it over," but a full devotion of love and self-giving by the husband for the wife. What more perfect pattern for marriage could there be, she asks: "Who can improve on the love of Christ for us?" (Achtemeier, 1976, p. 86).

In a remarkable way this understanding of headship overcomes the negative consequences of the curse. If the curse created an imbalance of power, then for a husband to love his wife and give himself up for her means taking the initiative in righting the imbalance. In other words, "headship" means taking primary responsibility to nurture the full restoration of a woman's freedom to thrive as an equal partner.

Mutual submission then will be expressed by the husband in loving service to empower his wife. The wife will express her submission in respect appropriate towards one who puts *her* well-being above his own. Whether the marriage appears to be a traditional one with clear-cut roles or a nontraditional one, where these dynamics are at work, there will be a balanced grace, a mutual welcome reminiscent of Eden (Stevens, 1989, p. 154).

The marvel of the Genesis account, pointed out by Achtemeier, is that the writer, despite laws and customs of the entire ancient Near East in that day, could look beyond the structure of his own society and see that the subordination of woman was not God's original intent, but the result of our sin. It is beyond rational explanation how the writer could grasp that, instead of the wholesome oneness God had planned, the rule of man over woman was a distortion, a consequence of our proud attempt to live out our lives apart from God. It flies in the face of all customs and beliefs in civilizations of the ancient world, and still represents a totally unique position, she writes. The writer of Genesis must have been grasped by the most radical revelation of God's desire for his universe (Achtemeier, 1976, pp. 74-76). Today that vision returns us with renewed passion to Eden's delights of true marital companionship.

22.
The Marriage of Best Beloveds

Last week we celebrated Gerald's Halloween birthday. The boys orchestrated a treasure hunt. Their clues included word and number codes and puzzles for Dad to unravel. What fun to see even Dad stumped, at least momentarily. Grandpa and Grandma enlivened the party with stories of where and what they were up to at 38 years of age. Among other things, Grandma was giving birth to baby number eight, and Grandpa was receiving his B.D. (equivalent to M.Div.) degree. During our birthday liturgy, we all chose a verse or two of scripture to read for Gerald. Timothy chose James 1:2-4, evoking tears in his dad's eyes. The past months had been rough! "My brothers and sisters, whenever you face trials of any kind, consider it nothing but joy, because you know that the testing of your faith produces endurance; and let endurance have its full effect, so that you may be mature and complete, lacking in nothing" (NRSV).

The card that accompanied my gift read, "We've got a good thing going . . . and I love it . . . ."

Do we dare speak of marital in-love-ness in a public forum? Because marriage has received so much bad press, it seems not only urgent but imperative that those of us who usually fancy being married share that thrill abroad. Otherwise, who among our young people, in their right mind, would want to consider it?

The hard work that makes up our marriage has been daily and

sometimes agonizing. There have been at least as many lows as highs, but the highs have been the stuff of Life—the stuff that makes it all infinitely worthwhile. And the bond of loyalty has created a secure place in which to bring even the ugliest parts of ourselves to be embraced and healed.

Then the Lord God said, "It is not good that the man should be alone. I will make him a helper as his partner" (Genesis 2:18 NRSV). There is no word spoken by God more merciful than this one, spoken at the beginning, writes Elizabeth Achtemeier in *The Committed Marriage*. In an age when we seem to have turned in on ourselves and salvation has come to be understood as development of an independent "personhood," God's plan for partnership speaks to the deepest hungers of our hearts. God intends that we live in relationship with another! What a great mercy! (Achtemeier, 1976, pp. 11-12).

A paean of praise to two lovers who thrill to each other is sung in the Song of Solomon. These poetic stanzas sing of the ecstasy of intimacy. Yet, writes Donald Joy in *Bonding*, intimacy between lovers cannot but speak of more. It is a human experience that reflects something eternal. "Hold me tight" is our persistent human cry—but ultimately it is a gesturing toward God the parent, God the lover. Intimacy is the ultimate human yearning and destiny—to "know as we are known," both "naked and unashamed" (Joy, 1985, pp. 176-178).

And there is a lovely interdependence in the trusting embrace of two who have covenanted to protectively hold one another "for better or for worse." Even as a man feels compelled to care for his wife while she suckles and cares for a child, he also in weakness draws strength from her tender embrace. Joy suggests that while he suckles her breast, he says in effect, "I have always known that while I must protect you . . . I will always draw my strength from you. I depend on you. You don't know how weak and dependent I feel. But you make me strong. . ." What we know about a man's need for sexual intimacy, Joy continues, tells us something about who may be the weaker sex. A male is quite fragile, he asserts, and tends not to thrive as well as a female when left alone (Joy, 1985, p. 52).

"Hold me tight!"—the heart cry of everyone born. Recent images on our TV news of one baby found in a trash bin and another in the washing machine at a laundromat stab us to the heart. The babies' cries, "Hold me tight," gave away their whereabouts. The need to be held tightly is something we never outgrow. It simply takes different forms as we grow into adulthood.

Intimacy points toward more, far more, than physical embrace. It yearns toward something ultimate, something eternal. "The current campaign for 'safe sex' suggests intimacy with no risk," writes *Washington Post* columnist Colman McCarthy (Nov. 16, 1991), "as if beginning a relationship is on the level of a handshake.

". . . To narrow sex to the anatomical is to trivialize it," he writes. "The human need to love and be loved instinctively wants more. Safe sex in the '90s is as bogus a goal as free love in the '60s. . . . The young deserve better. They are more than their genitals."

The yearning for intimacy that ultimately draws us toward our maker is at heart a mystical yearning.

Most of us down-to-earth folk need daily hand and body reminders that we're held firmly in a loving embrace, that we haven't slipped through the everlasting fingers. God's great merciful gift of covenanted love between a man and a woman incarnates, perhaps most profoundly, God's covenant of love with each of us, for better or for worse.

23.
*We're Traditional Folk—
And That's Just Fine*

We were determined, Gerald and I, that our wedding would be anything but *traditional*. There would be no bridesmaids or grooms-men, no elaborate costumes, no lengthy sermon or standard vows, no wedding cake. We even refused all but one or two posed photos (there were plenty of action shots) lest it appear, as in so many other weddings, that all the fixings were meant for spectacle. After the wedding was over, someone wondered aloud if and when we had gotten married. No authority had made the public statement pronouncing us "husband and wife"!

The irony, as I reflect now some 16 years later, is that I am today frequently invited to speak on the importance of family rituals and traditions. Tradition, instead of remaining a bad word, has become a term I reverence and use respectfully. Last week we watched "Fiddler on the Roof" again for the first time in many years. I grieved as I hadn't earlier for the papa who struggles so gracefully and valiantly to be faithful to the wisdom of his ancestors while exhibiting a measure of sensitivity to the real desires of his own daughters.

The lyrical music of the fiddler, precariously balanced on the peak of the roof, carries on undeterred through all the upheaval. It re-minded me of one favorite song: "My life flows on in endless song, above earth's lamentations; I catch the sweet, though far-off hymn that hails the new creation. Through all the tumult and the strife, I hear that music ringing. It finds an echo in my soul. How can I keep from singing?"

In looking more closely at our wedding, I now find that it was, in truth, deeply traditional. We eliminated the superficial fluff—trappings that, though conventional, convey little content other than display of finery and form. The traditions that we honored, almost despite ourselves, drew most profoundly on that which has shaped the real content of marriages for generations—the blessing of the gathered community on our union, the heavy reliance on scriptural wisdom both in sharing by our parents and in our own reflection, and the content of our public commitments to each other. We tapped into the very heart of our faith tradition, even while imagining we were being so untraditional.

Our "vows" read:

On this day, in the presence of all of you, we—Gerald and Sara—commit ourselves to extend the trust and joy our families have taught us into a home of our own.

We will be loving and honest mirrors to each other's gifts and growth.

We will share in the freedom and newness of life in Christ.

In choosing each other today, we promise to continue making that same choice, whatever the changes time may bring.

As members of a Kingdom beyond this earth, we will be strangers and transients in a world that does not know Christ; but we commit ourselves to establish a homeland of the heart.

And finally we give ourselves as full partners for life, in service to each other in our home, and to others in our world.

Reviewing now the words we hammered out late that night before the wedding under the tremendous pressure to be original (to reinvent the wheel), I marvel. So much of how I conceive of myself and our relationship today was captured in those words written by two immature, arrogant young adults! The integrity and power of our faith tradition, while conveyed mostly in words then, has since grown into the heart and fiber of our relationship.

To promise to carry on the goodness of our own homes into a new home was to admit to a desire for continuity with a tradition that had made us who we are. Honesty and integrity have been a cornerstone of our communication, both between ourselves and within the community of believers. The desire for a vital spirituality is interwoven into all that we do. And that our commitment to each other would be characterized by the act of choosing each other over and over again, rather than a once and done decision, acknowledged the fact that 25 years later we would not be the same persons who married each other way back then. Little did we know how precious a lifelong commitment would seem in our generation.

Recognizing ourselves at that early stage as part of a people in exile indicated more accurately than we knew, our self-understanding as counter-culture Christians. Our work together has compelled us to wander in distant places. Now, 16 years and some 12 households later, I treasure that "homeland of the heart" more than I ever realized possible. Truly to be at home with God, and at home with one's people stretching over boundaries and over centuries, is the dearest of homelands.

And finally, in what appears, though subtly, to be a flagrant rebuttal of tradition we committed ourselves to a marriage of equal partners, a marriage in which our roles would be characterized not by hierarchy but by personal gifts and mutual service. And even in this, through years of discernment, we've discovered a strong tradition honoring what we understand to be the biblical model for married partners, rather than the distorted patterns of husband over wife that have sometimes characterized what passed for Christian marriage.

And so we are very traditional folk after all—perhaps radically so—but traditional nonetheless.

24.
Fathers: An Endangered Species

On Father's Day this year, the father of our three was on the other side of the ocean. The children and I were visiting in my parents' home over the weekend of that noteworthy day. All I could think of was my own children's father and how none of us had had sufficient foresight to put a card in the mail in time to reach him on that day. Perhaps he won't remember it's Father's Day, I comforted myself. They don't celebrate such a day in Croatia so there won't be any advertisements jumping off the pages of the newspaper or gift suggestions leaping off the shelves to remind him that we've forgotten. And suddenly it occurred to me that I'd forgotten to prepare any remembrance for my own father near at hand, or for my husband's father across town. Oh well, I reasoned. It's such a commercialized day. They all know we love them. I don't need to be compulsive about reminding them.

It took the words of Ellen Goodman, newspaper columnist, to shake me from my lethargy that Father's Day morning before church. It suddenly felt heartless of me to take our fathers for granted. The children and I moved in a flurry of inspired activity gathering flowers and writing cards to honor those who have so profoundly blessed our lives. We placed a surprise phone call to our dearly beloved thousands of miles away and caught him exhausted after three weeks of intensive lecturing and preaching, poring through piles of student papers in eight different languages.

The children sang him a song, and by turns told him they miss him and love him. He could hardly speak for tears. The impact of a surprise gift of love across the miles when he was feeling particularly lonely buoyed him for a few tender moments.

Father's Day used to be a salute to the "solid souls who brought home the bacon," writes Goodman. But today it carries a different message. Now, "the socially approved images of fatherhood are emotional, not financial. They are about love, not money."

She cites James Levine, director of the Fatherhood Project, on what fathers really want. First and foremost they want to be "the providers, the economic and physical protectors of their families. That's how men feel at a gut level and it's what women expect," he said. "Second of all, they want a different relationship with their children than they had with their own father."

Our grandparents, writes Goodman, counted themselves success-ful if they provided well for their children. But today, "we count our success as parents by what we do *with* our children. So fathering is less about a role and more about a relationship." Today, we expect intimacy. When we measure the quality of family life, we look at the feelings we have for each other—the love bonds that are formed and sustained. Being a father is a "high maintenance job"—more layered, with heightened expectations, and not as clear-cut as bringing home the bacon used to be.

The widespread longing for relationship with one's children speaks of a severe father deprivation that has characterized the life of families since industrialization plucked fathers out of their homes and small family businesses. The physical and psychological absence of fathers from their families has been called "one of the great underestimated tragedies of our times," its dimensions too vast for quick analysis.

Inasmuch as fathers are coming home again, not only with the bacon, but to hold, talk and play *with* their children, they are on the road to recovery, and Father's Day is well worth celebrating. Perhaps by acknowledging what a rare species loving, respectful, stalwart fathers have become, we will come to esteem them with new grati-tude. The fragility of the father-family bond in our time requires on

Father's Day and every day sober reflection on what it takes to be a successful father.

When I think of how my father determined early on, even before the trend had reached measurable proportions, that he would be emotionally available to his children in a way that his father hadn't been for him, I want to celebrate. When my own children's father, even though physically distant on Father's Day, communicates so that his children know without a doubt that he cherishes them, and, when on his return they each run with unsuppressed joy into his arms, I want to celebrate. A good father is hard to find.

25.
Where's Dad—
And God the Father?

Last Saturday was a crisp, heartbreakingly beautiful autumn day. Leaves swirled, dancing with the wind. The earth, even when robed in its death shroud, exuded vitality. With an unexpected free day on his hands, Gerald donned grubby jeans and jacket to set about chopping wood for our winter stove. After finishing their weekly housecleaning, the boys headed out to join Dad, cajoled into it despite the freezing temperatures. Both were soon wielding the axe, coached by Dad and encouraged with cups of hot chocolate from Mom. Little sister, who had labeled herself "Daddy's helper" early on, stood by to pick up the scraps. Obvious satisfaction radiated from each face as the blade splintered seasoned logs into usable chunks.

It was a priceless morning. Opportunities for father and sons to work side by side are too few at our house. They play a lot of games together, spend time reading, eating and talking together, but "real work" is usually parceled out away from home—yours at your school, mine at my school. One wonders how other lifestyle choices might have offered more day-to-day, hands-on opportunities to model skills and values. But it's a little late in the game for wistful thinking. And who is to say that what we do best around home isn't "real work"—activities related to words and numbers, music and analysis of world events, computers and reasoning skills, books and more books?

Yet there is still something magical about chopping wood with Dad that doesn't quite compare with matching wits on a word game. Something elemental. Something in tune with the heartbeat of nature and the seasons. Something that engages one's whole vibrant body. To deprive sons of the opportunity to test their skills against Dad's, to be coached and encouraged by him in a whole array of activities, is to deprive them of a fundamental birthright.

But father-deprivation isn't only about work. "Lots of baby-boomer fathers are self-congratulatory when they compare themselves to the dads of the 1950s," comments David Blankenhorn, president of the Institute for American Values, in *The Washington Post*. "But even if they were emotionally distant, those '50s dads weren't morally distant. They were home every night. Not enough of today's dads are around their kids enough to be a moral presence."

Due in part to the tripling of the divorce rate and the quadrupling of the out-of-wedlock birthrate, the *Post* observes, men aged 20-49 spend an average of only seven years living in a house with young children, a decline of nearly 50 percent in the past 30 years. "At the neighborhood level, when you have lots of households where fathers are not present, the whole social order breaks down," notes Mercer Sullivan, researcher in New York. "Teenagers take over the streets."

The same article cites Robert Bly's book, *Iron John*. "The love unit most damaged by the Industrial Revolution has been the father-son bond," he writes. *Iron John's* charge to the top of the bestseller list seems to confirm that fatherhood is suffering from an identity crisis. Bly argues that when work and home became spatially separated a century ago, boys stopped experiencing firsthand the work their fathers did. Many picked up their mother's disapproving view of masculinity; others compensated for their father's absence by becoming hypermasculine and violence-prone.

The "father-involved" family is a fragile cultural achievement and cannot be taken for granted, writes John Miller in *Biblical Faith and Fathering*. Fathering is culturally acquired to a greater extent than mothering is. A mother's relationship to the child is more obvious from the start. Not so with the father, who may not even be able to ascertain whether a child is actually his own. Consequently, when a culture ceases to support a father's involvement with his own children (through its laws, mores, symbols, models, rituals), powerful natural forces take over in favor of the mother-alone family (Miller, 1989, pp. 5,13). Miller's warning becomes an alarm when viewed in light of statistics. A *Washington Post* article (February 2, 1991) reports that there are 9.7 million single parents in the nation, 41% more than a decade earlier. Nearly all the single parents are women.

One is compelled to ask, how have we as a culture so dramatically failed to support a father's involvement with his family? The answer is many-faceted. One could quote the experts forever. The voices crying to be heard on all sides are giving me a severe case of whiplash.

From one direction I hear that calling God "Father" all these centuries has created a distortion of who God is. We would do well, the argument goes, to wipe our mental slates clean of such a male-dominated, patriarchal misnomer. Blame for our abuse of the environment and of each other is laid at the feet of a distant, autocratic Father-God. And men have over-inflated their macho egos by identifying with such a lord-king-ruler God, wreaking havoc in family relationships.

It has usually been women who point out this male bias in our traditional thinking about God. In doing so, they have spoken a prophetic word. There has been gross misuse of god labels and concepts. When men have dominated our culture and dominated our teaching about God, it is no wonder that we have received a lopsided view. In an age when we have plundered and polluted the earth to our own peril, it seems only appropriate that we reexamine our concepts of God as mostly other—a judge and overlord. To recover a sense of the intimacy and warmth of a mothering God is a prophetic corrective in our day. But where does that leave fathers, who are already dangling with a severe identity crisis? If "father" has become synonymous with tyrant, the word is completely gutted of its true meaning and becomes a self-fulfilling prophecy.

And then my head is jerked in another direction. From another quarter comes the insight that only in the biblical stories (in contrast to other ancient myths) is there a divine father who is a major force for good in the world (Miller, pp. 41-43). In contrast to other father gods of the ancient Near East, this father god is worthy of respect, is fully in charge of the cosmic home and is good, asserts Miller. And I also hear the suggestion that it wasn't only happenstance that Jesus made fatherhood a central feature. By relating to God as "Abba" (Papa), Jesus rejected the caricature of an arbitrary, autocratic "Father." He demonstrated instead, by his life and teaching, that the heart of the gospel is a suffering God, who, like a loving father, takes the children into his arms and lays down his life for them. In this may lie the relevance of the Bible, suggests Miller (p 52). It undergirds and encourages human fathers, because it illustrates a firm belief in God as an effectively *caring* father (pp. 58, 78).

There are solid reasons for thinking that the biblical representation of God as caring father has had a generally humanizing effect in the lives of both men and women, Miller continues. Fathers in Israel consequently obtained for themselves an identity as redemptive caretakers with an ongoing, permanent stake in the life of their families. Jewish family rituals and festivities reinforced the father's significant role in the family.

Father religion is more important for men than mother religion is for women, argues Miller, because mothering is a biologically determined experience far more than fathering. Since nature has invested mothers with such power and prominence in the life cycle, culture must intervene on behalf of fathers if they are to be significantly and even equally involved. This, in part, underlines the significance of calling God "Father" (Miller, p. 135).

Even as I whip back and forth to catch the drift of this debate, I wonder whether there aren't elements in both perspectives that, when intertwined, strengthen each other rather than contradict each other. The involvement of many more women in teaching the Bible and preaching has opened our eyes and hearts to the mothering faces of God, so that our God is experienced in expanded dimensions of warmth, diversity and beauty. But also, and perhaps now more urgently in an age of father-deprivation, it seems imperative to speak freely about the compassionate, liberating Father-God shown throughout scripture. Not the caricature. We do our fathers and our God a tremendous disservice if we allow all that has gone wrong with the abuse of authority to tarnish what was meant to be—a father who dynamically acts to protect and sustain his family even as a mother beside him does so in *her own* dynamic way.

26.
Father-Mother God

> *O that you would tear open the heavens and come down, so that*
> *the mountains would quake at your presence. . .*
>
> *When you did awesome deeds that we did not expect, you came*
> *down, the mountains quaked at your presence. From ages past no*
> *one has heard, no ear has perceived, no eye has seen any God besides*
> *you, who works for those who wait for him. . . .*
>
> *O Lord, you are our Father; we are the clay and you are the*
> *potter; we are all the work of your hand. Do not be exceedingly*
> *angry, O Lord, and do not remember iniquity forever.*
>
> (Isaiah 64:1, 3, 4, 8, 9a NRSV)

Isaiah 64 reads as a piercing, desperate appeal, the cry of a person on the edge of despair. Oh, that you would rend the heavens and come down! We've heard stories of the way you used to show yourself in dramatic displays of power. Come again! Shatter the status quo. Pronounce the day of our liberation!

This is a cry born of a stubborn faith that God is able to help. No apathetic acquiescence to the way things are. If it's an impersonal, evil universe, the only alternative really is to give up. But *No!* protests our ancient ancestor.

Since ancient times no one has heard or seen the kind of God that you are, who *acts* on behalf of those who wait on you. Show yourself again, as you have been known to do. Don't abandon us. Yes, we have sinned and made you angry. Even our righteousness is as filthy rags. But you are a God who saves. We know it from story after story of the way you have intervened on behalf of your people.

And because you *are* a God who saves, I'm going to count on it and stubbornly sit here waiting to see your salvation work its way out.

This is a cry to a God who is personal. It is not a cry to a distant deity, a force that set the universe in motion and then drifted off into interstellar space. It is not an appeal to a nature god, a spirit of trees or cliffs. It is a request to one known as "Father" and as a "potter" who shapes us and makes us what we are.

And for that very reason, pleads Isaiah, because you father us and shape us into a work of art, because you are that kind of God, don't be angry beyond measure. Don't remember our sins forever. Come near to us and save us.

In a day when it appears we may be on our way to a "fatherless society," and the church grapples with the new realities of a post-patriarchal world, it seems imperative to look more closely at the character of God's fatherly love for people. It seems that we have made of God an absent, autocratic, whip-wielding, unfeeling lord. Such a caricature tells more about how we experienced our own distant fathers than it describes the divine fathering exemplified in the stories of God's people. That Isaiah would appeal to God—because of your *fathering* don't be angry beyond measure but come near and save— speaks not of a father who is an autocratic overlord, but of a father who shows loving care for the well-being of children.

It must have felt like a daring presumption to claim a family connection with the transcendent God of the heavens—and yet what more liberating, ecstatic claim could there be! The people of Israel were familiar with nature worship and with their dependence on nature. Encounters with Mother Earth and with the suckling nurturing of mothers were a daily reality. To learn that God also transcends nature, and can radically change one's situation by entering to liberate and save, awakened a new reality. That God as father would care for children—sheltering, feeding, binding up wounds—wove the concept of fatherhood-as-intimate-involvement-in-the-lives-of-one's-family into the Israelites' minds in a radical new way, providing a model for all fathers.

Our longing for more images of God as mother, for more ways of experiencing God up close—within us and within the natural world—speaks more of our alienation in this age of enlightenment than it does of a need to radically remake the biblical witness to the character of God. Throughout much of history, the images of mother-love have been more accessible than those of father-love. That the God of Israel would become known primarily as a father-God elevated father-love as it was meant to be—nurturing, guiding, liberating. To reembrace our own nearness to nature and the God who is Spirit, animating all life, we do not need to reject the father-character of God. If we have rested in the arms of a mothering Spirit, allowing ourselves to be nursed and rocked, we will be prepared to welcome a father's arms to lift us and give us a vision beyond the encircling arms. If we can know the shelter of a mother's womb, the relief of her milk, and also come to know the entrance of a father's firm embrace, we can experience early on the glorious interplay of mother *and* dad. It is to know the intermingling of styles and colors in infinite variations and to revel in the strength and beauty of being complementary, the image of God in father and mother.

27.
Women and Men, Servants Together

Erisman Mennonite Church recently celebrated a centennial of its meetinghouse with a weekend of festivities and special guests. Gerald was invited to reflect on what it was like growing up in that particular church family. He took his two sons along for the four-hour trip, to be present at his home church's trip down memory lane. I stayed home, since it was my turn to preach at our own congregation. Recent frequent absences made it imperative that I be present.

Of course, when only part of the family showed up at Erisman's, Gerald met the frequent question, "Where is Sara?" He replied, "She couldn't come because she's preaching this morning in Harrisonburg."

"Do you know what one man said?" indignant Joseph reported later. "He asked Daddy, 'Is she taking *your* place?' And he wasn't the only one who asked."

"No," Gerald had responded, "she's taking *her* place."

The debate over men and women in church leadership has been explosive in our generation—a family quarrel that still smolders. The victims of the quarrel are too many to count. At some few moments, I've been on the front line. Usually I've watched from a distance while others engaged up close. But always, I've wanted to make sense of it all.

Elizabeth Achtemeier acknowledges in *The Committed Marriage* that the church has always had trouble living up to its own gospel. "Paradoxically, no institution has been more reluctant to grant equal rights to women than has the body of Christ itself," she writes. "We deny our gospel before the cynical eyes of the world when we deny freedom of status and function to any person, male or female. . . . We have too often proclaimed a gospel that we have not lived, as not only the women but also the blacks, the poor, the social outcasts can readily attest. . . . Failing to stand fast in its freedom, the church has continually submitted to new yokes of slavery" (Achtemeier, 1976, p. 80).

It has been energizing to watch God empowering women for ministry in a new way. It has forced me to seriously consider what the call of God is in my life when laziness and irresponsibility are two of my gravest temptations. I am tempted to hide—to want my husband to create a life for me. But the Spirit has convicted me time and again, has prodded me to take the risk of responsible investment of my own gifts.

The new wine of the Spirit requires new wineskins. The leadership model wherein a group of men, by virtue of their maleness, are seen as a notch above others, as authoritative "heads," is no longer a life-giving model. This pattern has too often given us women who are easily tempted toward unhealthy dependency and irresponsibility. It has also caused us to elevate visible roles above others because those roles have been the exclusive right of a group of men. Rather than enabling us to grow up to full maturity in Christ, this model serves more powerfully to keep some of us immature. Structured into the very center of church life is the paternalistic reminder that we (women) can never hope to be equal partners with the men "on top," no matter how much we grow up in Christ. On this model, only a few males, by virtue of their spiritual authority, perhaps, but also their gender, are fit to teach the scriptures and lead public worship. It is no wonder that many women did not find Christianity to be good news and looked elsewhere for affirmation that their femaleness is of value. I know the argument that excluding women from some church leadership roles doesn't reflect on their essential worth. But it does! And in the church most of all, because we are *co-heirs* of all the abundant gifts and freedoms that belong to the children of God.

Why is the question of a woman's identity within the church an issue with me? Some women have problems with males in leadership because of bad experiences with fathers and husbands. I have problems with exclusively male leadership because of good experiences with men. "Male headship" has meant, for me, the *restoration* of full equality to women, where mutuality becomes a way of life, so that one cannot comprehend why one should be excluded on the basis of gender. It is precisely because I have been loved and valued as a daughter, as a wife, as a sister, as a mother and as a woman that I cannot easily hear that my gender makes me any less worthy than a man to serve in any way.

When women are excluded from certain kinds of leadership in the church, one result is to make us despise ourselves as women. Such exclusion forces us to imagine that we must become like men to merit God's anointing. The highest esteem is shown for our *womanness* when room is made for our full participation in church life.

Excluding women from church leadership also has repercussions for children. Any structure that reflects the view that women are somehow unfit to serve as pastors or teachers has the effect of degrading that which women *are* permitted to do, namely child care. As long as women are not seen in visible, public roles other than mother or Sunday school teacher, younger men and women are led to believe that child care is somehow less significant, because that's all women may do. When child care and homemaking are an integral part of a variety of women's and men's flourishing ministries, they become an asset, positively affecting the character of leadership in general.

Men and women—servants together. We have seen what it means for Christlike men to love "even unto death," to respect and value women so thoroughly that they will make room for women to function as full-fledged partners in ministry. And we have seen Christlike women, who dare to shoulder responsibility and partner with men, bringing the unique strengths they have as women to correct traditional male biases in leadership.

In our home and our work as co-pastors, we talk about mutual respect and support. I respect my husband's ministry and care for him when he feels weak; he respects my ministry and cares for me when I feel weak. It is not one above another, but each helping to create an environment where the other can thrive. There are crises he is better equipped to handle. There are crises I am better equipped to handle. "The buck stops" with him at one time, and with me at another, as we share responsibility together to discern and do God's will.

Where the Spirit of the Lord is, there is freedom. It is clear from the biblical witness and the history of the church that God anoints women for leadership in the family of God. If God does this, how dare we structure women rigidly out of leadership? Unless we take arbitrary measures to make leadership distinctions based on gender, the Spirit raises up men *and* women to lead us. Our leadership then more completely reflects the image of God and the will of God in creating us male and female in the beginning. God made us different so that each has something unique to give. Our distinctiveness as male and female is the strongest reason for men *and* women to participate *together* in all aspects of church and home life—servants together.

V.

Renewal at Home

28.
The Celebrative Life

We've often heard of the celibate life, the contemplative life, the monastic life but what is the celebrative life?

When our children began graduating from babyhood and distinguishing between mother's milk and birthday cake, we began to ask the little questions. How shall we celebrate birthdays? Shall we have a Christmas tree? What song shall we sing at the breakfast table?

And then came the bigger questions. How do children develop a sense of identity that runs deeper than the latest fad? How do we cultivate home-based traditions that enhance family spirit and stability, linking us with generations gone by? What sort of religious traditions, values and world view do we want to instill in our children?

My questions led me into the homes of numerous families in the Reba Place Church community near where we were living, and the result was a book entitled *Why Not Celebrate!*, a gift from a group of people who have struggled for years with what it means to be family and church in modern, urban America. It was a life-giving inquiry for me and has enriched our family life, making us more deliberate about the traditions and celebrations we cultivate.

One might ask, why work so deliberately at establishing traditions—those celebrations and rituals that tell us who we are no matter where we are? Don't traditions just get passed from generation to generation almost without thought? Don't we have a Christmas tree or go to church on Sunday or have turkey for Thanksgiving just because that's the way it's always been in our homes?

Traditions come from many sources—cultural inheritance, religious heritage, and those that a particular family creates on its own. We can do things sort of willy-nilly, drifting unreflectively through traditions that come from here and there and everywhere, or we can start early as a family to shape a life together that reflects who we are, where we've come from and where we want to go.

We can't assume our children will figure out who they are and what direction they want to take if we just give them a grab bag of traditions we've haphazardly thrown together.

We have to ask ourselves, what values do we truly honor? How do we tell our children who they are and where they fit into the kaleidoscope of cultures and religions stretched around the world?

Either we take our directions from the loudest, most persuasive voices in the mass media, or we are nurtured by centuries of traditional stories and symbols that have guided countless families through prosperity and adversity. Either we lamely follow the most dominant trends hyped by sales pitches all around us, or we select a style of life together that is informed from a treasure trove of family memories, traditional stories and ways of being that enrich and deepen our well-being.

To celebrate life means, in part, to reject the temptation to become mere passive consumers. It means to deliberately structure life so as to be able to delight in the cycles and the seasons, the beginnings and the endings, the rhyme and the reason of it all. It means believing that life's everyday and eternal dimensions are filled with purpose. If children can be shown God's graceful patterns interwoven throughout history and our daily life, they will want to celebrate with us.

29.
Exiles, Even at Home

Remember today that your children were not the ones who saw and experienced *the discipline of the Lord your God: his majesty, his mighty hand, his outstretched arm; the signs he performed and the things he did in the heart of Egypt. . .* It was not your children who saw what he did for you in the desert until you arrived at this place . . . But it was your own eyes that saw all these great things the Lord has done.

Fix these words of mine in your hearts and minds; tie them as symbols on your hands and bind them on your foreheads. Teach them to your children, *talking about them when you sit at home and when you walk along the road, when you lie down and when you get up. Write them on the door frames of your houses and on your gates, so that your days and the days of your children may be many in the land that the Lord swore to give your forefathers, as many as the days that the heavens are above the earth.*

(Deuteronomy 11:2,3a,5,7,18-21
NIV, emphasis added)

More than likely the most significant reason we have a rich Judeo-Christian heritage today is the one pointedly repeated in Deuteronomy 11: it was not your children who saw, so teach them, show them, draw it for them, sing the stories to them when you sit at home, when you walk, when you lie down. God established festivals for remembering—Passover, the Sabbath, the Feast of Tabernacles, the Year of Jubilee. The people of Israel were instructed to build altars for remembering, to craft an ark of the covenant and fill it with symbols for remembering.

The people of God have, through generations of faithful retelling, bequeathed to us a history filled with landmarks and dramatic displays of God's intervention in human affairs. When for a generation or two we drift off into legalisms or headtrips, that history, as long as we continually reacquaint ourselves with it, tugs us back into line. Or when we drift into some extreme or popular philosophy, thinking the revelation we've received today is superior to all that has gone before, the stories of God's people serve to correct and realign us. Retelling the stories of God's work throughout history keeps us from the arrogance of our own near-sighted egos.

It was essential for the people of God to keep telling the stories because they were often refugees, exiles in a foreign land. They had to keep telling the stories of Abraham and Sarah leaving their homeland, of the Exodus from oppression in Egypt, of David and Esther—to remember—because generation after generation they experienced massive dislocations, wars, persecutions, and the constant temptation toward assimilation with neighboring cultures and religions.

As the people of God today we are also exiles in a foreign land. As exiles we must draw significant strength and direction from a faith history that shapes us and names us. We live in constant culture shock amid our present realities.

Exiles can't take their identity as a people for granted. Ethnic groups that move willingly or forcibly into a foreign country cling tenaciously to their own identifiable patterns because their identity is constantly threatened. So it is with us. Even though we may never have moved from our hometown, our loyalty to the Kingdom of God identifies us as a people in exile, a people who need constantly to find our bearings in a rapidly changing world.

Not only as individuals, but as families, as churches, as entire denominations we experience the strains of culture shock and the disorientation and identity conflicts accompanying it. Very quickly in the midst of changes we find ourselves adrift on a sea, forgetting where we've come from and where we are going.

I personally have been through frequent culture changes. Sometimes I feel that my entire life has been lived in culture shock, both as the child of missionary parents and as an adult in a variety of cultural settings. The many moves have taken their emotional toll. One of the more significant reasons we've been able to weather the various upheavals, both in my childhood family and now in my own family, is that we've built up a cluster of traditions and stories that tell us who we are no matter where we are.

As first-generation immigrants know so well, their children and grandchildren will more than likely want to blend in, learn the local language, adopt the local customs. Those traditions, aromas and styles that evoke memories of the distant homeland will all too soon become only wisps of faint memory—a forgotten past.

An insight that has grown out of the Believers Church tradition is that as a people of faith rooted in history we are always only *one generation away from extinction.* Part of the genius of the biblical stories is that they have, more than any other body of literature, been embraced over and over again by successive generations who've found within them words of life for their day. If they hadn't been, our family of faith would have been an endangered species long ago.

This past summer was our son's first experience of summer camp at a church-affiliated campground. On hearing that there would be Bible study during the week, he groaned. His groan hit my anxiety button. Why was he upset? Was it because Bible study sounded too much like school, or had his exposure to the Bible in Sunday school or elsewhere already turned him off? I took the opportunity to talk with him (lecture him?!).

"Son," I told him, "this world is a crazier place than ever, and a pretty scary place. Many of your friends don't have a clear sense of purpose or direction. Whether you believe it or not, this study is a privilege. Whether you learn to love it or not, I want you to know the Bible has been a profound help to many, many people, and also to me.

"It's as if we are on a hill that is eroding, faster and faster, and if some of us don't put down roots and hold on, we'll lose our footing.

If some of us don't keep our bearings, we'll all be swept away. Son, we are the kind of people who are determined to keep our bearings, not in a rigid, unbending way, but in rehearsing over and over again who we are and where we've come from."

Fortunately, the Bible study was at fireside led by someone who breathed life and color into the stories. Our son came home with a light heart rather than a groan. With the weight of a faith history centuries old and still pulsating with life, how can we as parents ever hope to faithfully celebrate and pass it on? If we can't do it in a way that is life-giving, we will be one generation closer to extinction as a people of God.

30.
Rebuilding the Roof

We awoke one Monday morning and saw a crew of madmen ripping off our neighbors' roof, tearing it to shreds and deliberately exposing the small wooden house to the elements. When I showed our two-year-old Greta what was going on, hoping the action would divert her and allow me to get to my work, she looked with alarm at our own roof, and worried aloud that we might be next. "But I like our roof!" she objected, and was not at all entertained by the activity on the neighbors' roof.

We'd known the neighbors were hoping to expand their living space by adding a second story (rather than expanding on the ground level). But it is unnerving to watch the roof being torn off a house in which people and all their belongings still reside. I even dreamed that an enormous deluge of rain washed the vulnerable little house off its foundations and across the road into a green, soggy meadow.

And then what did the builders do after so deliberately ripping off the roof? They turned right around a couple days later and built another roof. To be sure, it's not the same roof. It's newer, and it's a whole story higher than the old one. But it's a roof, nonetheless.

I see an analogy for the way we relate, in successive generations, to faith and family traditions. In a sense, every family and each individual must put up their own new roofs. There is newness and continuity in this analogy. The materials are new, the structure is different, but the idea of the roof is passed from generation to generation. And interestingly enough, the foundation and basic walls of the house remain the same.

The roof that we must have over our heads is a legacy from the past to shelter us from the arrogance of thinking that today's world is all that ever existed. We expose ourselves to blustery, cruel storms if we forget our history and the traditions that have nurtured families for millennia. But we also do ourselves a terrible disservice if we fail to take those traditions and make them our own—reclaim them, rename them, rebuild them to characterize who we are in our own generation.

One tradition important within my own church family is that of foot-washing, exemplified by Jesus during his last supper with his disciples. When my family returned to what might be called a "very traditional" Mennonite community after many years of mission service in Ethiopia, I was 12 years old. Going to a foot-washing ceremony was an ordeal. Everyone but me knew exactly what to do. I stumbled along as all the women crowded into a small room to the right of the pulpit. I watched in disbelief as women hoisted up their skirts, undid their stockings, washed each others' feet (which they'd already washed and manicured with particular attention at home), gingerly kissed, and then put their stockings on again. (I noticed how some of the younger women shortcut the operation by simply washing and drying each other's stockinged feet.) The ritual was embarrassing for me, particularly since I knew it was meant to be profound.

Yet that "very traditional" Mennonite church gave me a roof. I have since rebuilt my roof and found foot-washing a truly profound ritual in other contexts, particularly in worship services at home or at a church Love Feast when we reenact Jesus' Last Supper.

We have several options as we shape our own family's faith traditions—and as we help to discern church family traditions. One is to pretend that we can survive without a roof—to discard in wholesale fashion anything that reminds us of the past we left behind. Another is to rebuild our roof but in a way that is architecturally disharmonious with the foundation and basic structure of the house. Or we can fashion a roof that suits our family's needs better than the old roof, but is fully harmonious with the structural integrity of the house.

31.
Falling in Love

My parents have a large bulletin board in their kitchen where they tack up recent photographs, news clippings, announcements and greeting cards. Upon my brother's graduation from Eastern Mennonite College, they posted the local paper's list of graduates and their majors. While visiting one day, a friend of my brother noticed his own name listed with a major in "Bible and Philosophy." "Bible!" he hooted. "BIBLE!" he laughed with no attempt to restrain his scorn. Apparently the young man had forgotten the official title of his declared major, originally selecting it only for the philosophy component. One can imagine that philosophy had seemed sufficiently sophisticated and intellectually superior to the biblical half of the program. Though the college had wedded the two, the distinction between Bible and philosophy was vitally important to this young scholar.

The incident, seemingly minor, remains riveted in my mind. Somehow in his derisive laugh I heard echoing many other snickers from friends and fellow students of my generation. I knew his was not an isolated scorn. Many of the Bible teachers and preachers of my growing-up years in denominational schools and churches did a tremendous disservice to the eloquence and awesome power of our faith story. I grieve with the memories of warped lives and ruined opportunities.

What went wrong for the young friend of my brother? He'd been raised in a devout Christian home and church where they had surely tried hard to pass on their faith. But there was something about the *way* the stories were told that brought scorn and not respect.

It seems to me that if we want our children to respect our faith commitments, the *way* we tell the story has everything to do with whether it is caught or rebuffed.

The first question we must ask ourselves is, "Are *we* sufficiently *in love* with our God and our faith story to win our children's desire to follow in the way?" *"In love"* is the key. Have the stories and traditions of our faith heritage captured our imaginations? Are we personally challenged and changed by them? Have the stories become a vital part of who we are, or do we merely repeat them as if there were some kind of magic in memorizing the content and woodenly reciting a progression of events? Do we talk about God and tell the stories of faith in all their mystery and drama, or do we manipulate them to bring a point home? To threaten and coerce? To inoculate our children with heavy indoctrination against evil?

Walter Wangerin writes in *The Manger is Empty*, "Faith should tell the tale. And love should serve it to the children lovingly. For it recounts no less than the beginning of the child's salvation. . . . Do you see? Do you see? The reason why the story must be told by a human mouth to human ears with human faith and affection is that a story is always more than information that some poor kid must labor to understand. A story is a world, my dears, both radiant and real—a world into which the child is invited, and she enters. . . . This, good parents, is the reason why you are telling your child the story, why you are weaving its marvelous world around her: because of love. Because you love her. . . . But also because you love the Lord. . . . But more than that, because the Lord Jesus loves your child; and how shall she know it except she also feels it?"

The story lives and vibrates—not because of hype, not because of forced enthusiasm, not because it's a "lesson to be learned." The story is reborn in each new generation because of love—our love for a faith that not only was, *but now is*, and will be forever, the heartbeat of Life!

In order to celebrate God and what it means to be a people of God we don't have to paint on happy faces and be bouncingly positive all the time. It simply means that we ourselves have been renewed by our own daily relationship with the Holy One so the stories ring true. Their truth and vibrancy cause us and our children to fall in love over and over again.

32.
Are We Really a Family?

One night at bedtime, Timothy said, "I spend a lot of time thinking, 'Am I really me?'" I smiled and remembered engaging in a similar reality check as a child. We talked a long time about all the messages we receive about who we are and who we should be and how confused we become in the process. Coming to know our unique identity and how it intersects with everything around us is a lifelong process.

Am I really me? Yes. But it often takes a lifetime to befriend that me, to name and honor the whole of me, and to celebrate even the brokenness that is me.

Another question follows on the heels of the first: are we really a family? If so, what kind of family? Who I am as an individual has a lot to do with how I see myself in family. What characterizes that family identity? Naming and celebrating our special uniqueness as a family (whether conventional, single-parent, blended) builds for family strength.

Rituals and traditions contribute immeasurably to shaping family identity. A child who reports with satisfaction that "our family likes to hike on the Appalachian Trail," or "our Dad makes scrumptious pizza every Friday night" is relaying her own joy in an identifying characteristic of her family. The traditions we choose will likely reflect our faith commitments, our cultural heritage in common with many others, as well as our own family flavor.

In different settings I've asked about traditions that were formative in shaping a person's sense of self and family. There are inevitably those that are common to many families—but also many that are unique to each family. Each family's combination of traditions builds a unique family identity and a sense of loyalty. Sitting down to talk about our traditions—whether cultural, religious or ones we've created ourselves—is a wonderful way to search out the threads that deliberately or serendipitously wove our own family tapestry.

In order for children to feel good about their family's traditions, they must have a sense of ownership. Children like to know that an event has not been imposed by parental authority, but that they too have some say in shaping it. They want to understand its inner logic. Perhaps it's about agenda for the "family meeting" each Wednesday at suppertime, or what to do for family fun night or family worship. The more input children have in shaping the event, confident that parental leadership will keep it on track, the more they will enjoy belonging to their own unique family.

One mother told how traditions her family has found most meaningful weren't begun deliberately; rather, an event together was so fine that everyone wanted to repeat it. A "tornado supper," for example, was the meal of hot dogs and sauerkraut they just happened to be having in Kansas when the sirens went off, warning them to retreat with supper in hand to the basement. Now whenever the weather is stirring up trouble, the children request their "tornado supper."

Another tradition set by a pastor and fondly recalled now by his grown son was for the whole family to go to the parlor (rarely used, almost a "holy" room in the house) each Sunday morning before church to read that Sunday's scripture.

We've found a weekly Sabbath meal on Saturday night to be a calming conclusion to the week and a welcome to the day of rest. We use a simple liturgy, with symbolic things to eat, family prayers, song and a hands-on blessing for each child. Our children miss the event if Mom or Dad feel we're too rushed or tired on a particular Saturday evening. It doesn't take a lot of extra effort. The structure is already there, with a time to worship together and bless each other, including anyone else who joins the circle. Even Greta, at three years, loves the experience. As Mom and Dad move around the circle laying hands on each child's head, she sits quietly with eager anticipation for her turn. We simply put hands on her head and pray a blessing—but for her it's pure delight.

A family Lenten tradition of giving up one small thing for the duration to remind us of Christ's supreme sacrifice is another we've adopted. Last year, before we'd begun to think about Lent together as a family, Timothy remembered. After major disappointment when he learned that a small-change offering each Sunday was going toward paying the church mortgage instead of aid to suffering ones in El Salvador, he thought and thought about what to do. Out of the blue he announced, "I know what I want to do for Lent. I want not to buy anything for myself during that time." A family tradition had taken root in his mind and served as the means by which he could express his heartfelt concern for the needs of others.

I'm not suggesting a new legalism when I talk about crafting a family identity to reflect who we uniquely are. Rather it is an invitation that every family, every single individual or household of persons actively cultivate events that embody values and delights that make us and our children glad to be who we really are.

33.
The Reliable Heartbeat of a Patterned Life

Whenever I tell Greta that it's too late—in fact it's way, way past normal bedtime—and so we don't have time to read our usual bedtime story, she throws a loud, tear-filled protest. It has taken repeated demonstrations to convince me that my logic, no matter how watertight, will not carry the day. In her mind it is *never* too late for a story. Sometimes I exercise parental fiat and force acquiescence, only to discover that the effort it took to make her buckle under was greater than sharing a story together, despite the hour. Lateness is hardly reason enough to rob her of her beloved bedtime pattern.

Children long for patterns like the reliable return of a cozy bedtime event or a cheerful holiday celebration. Like a warm blanket, repeated rituals securely wrap a child with rhyme and reason, with anticipation and fulfillment, over and over again. One can rest in its rhythm, knowing one is not forgotten, but reliably rocked morning to evening, weekend to weekend, year to year in a cradle of meaning.

Sometimes the patterns need to be changed as the children grow older or the composition of the family changes. One person reported in a *Christian Living* article (December 1989) that after a divorce in their family, the family traditions reminded them of happier times and were too painful, so nobody wanted to observe them. They decided rather than sitting in despair to start new patterns that would reflect their new reality.

Structures can be overhauled, rhythms changed, but there is the need to create a new pattern of meaningful activity to give the child the reassurance that though life has changed, there is still a reliable ebb and flow. All the verbal reassurances in the world will not be as comforting as some consistent pattern of being there for each other.

A patterned life can be as simple as agreeing to eat breakfast together, reading a verse of scripture or sharing a good-bye prayer and hug before heading out into the sometimes foreboding world of school and work. With the demise of family breakfasts we miss an invaluable opportunity to fortify our children for the enormous challenges they face each day at school—a disliked teacher, foul words used as weapons, and enough facts, figures and piles of homework to boggle an adult mind. The bowl of cereal and a "see you later" just don't suffice.

Another simple but disappearing tradition is having supper together. Sharon Johnson wrote in *Christian Living* (December 1989) on making the dinner hour a priority: "We live in an age when the American family is rapidly disintegrating. The dinner hour is the glue that holds our family together. It's a time to share sorrows and joys, and a time of fellowship. As we hold hands to pray, we bond with one another."

Newsweek (1990) reported that 56% of American families say they eat dinner together each evening. (Those who responded were only those found at home during the dinner hour.) Not bad, perhaps, but 40% of those do so with the TV or VCR on!

One pastor observed to me recently that he has visited homes that don't even have a gathering place for the whole family to come together for a meal at the same time. These families have no regular patterns for enjoying each other's company around food.

When I spoke to several public school elementary classes about traditions in their families and asked them to think of things they enjoy doing every day, it took a little pumping. Morning and bedtime traditions other than teeth-brushing seemed nonexistent. How about dinner together? About a third raised their hands. When I mentioned family vacations and Christmas traditions, hands sprouted all over the place. If teeth-brushing is the only activity most families do on a reliable pattern each day, we're in serious trouble! The tradition most children likely didn't think to mention is a myriad of television programs that simply must be consumed on a regular basis. Energy that might be invested in other regular activities together—such as a morning song, bedtime stories and prayer, for a bare minimum—all take second place to the electronic buzz of prime time.

I picked up a *McCall's* magazine the other day because its cover announced a feature on "Celebration Rituals to Strengthen Family Ties." It was the story of a mother determined to rebuild relationships with her adult children, feeling that many of their childhood years had been lost to traumas of divorce and her unhappy marriages. She instituted a tradition to strengthen family ties by providing a gourmet 11-course dinner for them each year, with an elaborately decorated table that took her three hours to set. She loved doing it and her children loved being so lavishly treated. But such an approach to traditions only serves to intimidate most of us and turn family events into ordeals rather than celebration.

Simplicity is the saving grace that allows me to mark time without madness. Gathering for a morning song, a short reading, a family hug at the door, or a bedtime story do not require elaborate preparations. They simply involve the committed desire to create a rhythm of meaning, a reassuring embrace of acted-out tender loving care for each other at home.

34.
Heroism of Nonconformity

During our years in Yugoslavia we learned that American film companies often come there to do their filming. The local film studio, Jadran, provided relatively inexpensive support crews, and in the countryside one could find a whole array of wonderful natural settings—ancient fortified castles, quaint villages, cobblestoned medieval ports, alpine mountains and the craggy, scenic Adriatic coast. From time to time Jadran Films called the American School, asking for English-speaking children to play small supporting roles in a variety of film projects.

One summer when American children were even scarcer than usual, Jadran called us for a toy commercial by Hasbro that needed American boys. After asking some questions and raising some possible objections, we agreed to meet for a conversation with the casting director when she arrived from New York.

The possibility of appearing in a movie is heady stuff. Some of the others at the school had already earned big bucks even for small parts. Joseph had earlier landed a speaking part in a film promoting tourism along the coast, earning $50 for a few hours of work. Some parents would be tickled to have their kids pull in a hefty sum doing cute things for commercials. We, however, didn't relish the prospect of our sons hawking some of the gruesome beasts and hideous contraptions that pass for toys these days.

This encounter called for some advance preparation with our sons. We weren't sure, we told them, what kind of toys would be in the commercials, but we wanted them to understand that it isn't all the same to us. We do have scruples, especially about violence. Money will not speak louder than other values we hold dear.

Meanwhile, we read up on the toy industry. The National Coalition on Television Violence listed Mattel, Kenner, *Hasbro* and Matchbox as manufacturers of the most violent toys. They further reported that the average American child will see over 800 advertisements promoting war toys in a year, along with some 250 episodes of cartoons produced for the explicit purpose of promoting war toys. During the period of 1982-85, the sale of war toys had increased by 600%, the Coalition declared.

The Hasbro casting director arrived. She needed "American-looking" kids for the G.I. Joe doll campaign. Because our Joseph seemed a likely fit, she took his photo. After she left, our family talked further. Can you stand with us? we asked Joseph. Are you willing to forego the money for this principle of ours?

Yes, he said, he was willing to give up the opportunity, though he hoped another would come again. We responded with a small compensation of our own, recognizing the cost of this sacrifice on his part. And graciously but firmly we declined further participation in the Hasbro project. Both boys were good sports about the whole affair. It was a teachable moment in our life together. We were grateful that our children had begun to catch the vision that life is more than chasing dollars—that there are some principles worth making sacrifices for.

The questions around money and what we do with it just don't go away. For parents and teens they only seem to grow more complex. I sometimes wonder if teens whom I know wouldn't be enormously pleased were the country wall to wall with shopping malls and video arcades.

I readily confess my aversion to Nintendo and similar gizmos. One more gadget that diverts a child from active involvement with the real world ought to be strenuously resisted. The hours invested in pushing buttons on electronic devices or vegetating in front of hot video screens are hours robbed from climbing trees, sculpting dinosaurs in snow or watching hawks wheel across the blue summer sky. Somehow in our obsession with providing our children with the latest trappings of the "good life," we give them far less while imagining that it is more.

A sister who lives with her family on a fruit and vegetable farm invited us over for supper this fall. Come early, she said, and we'll all husk and bunch Indian corn together to donate to the local thrift shop that raises money for a church relief organization.

I warmed immediately to the idea as a cooperative family project. On hearing the plan, the boys objected vehemently to having to work before running off with cousins to play. We persuaded them to give it a try, for at least a short while. Later while we all sat in a circle outside, enjoying the brisk fall air, the husking began. There were cries of delight as each corny ear emerged, displaying a unique multicolored mosaic. Soon there was no thought of disbanding. Each seemed eager to discover what the next ear of corn would look like. We exclaimed with amazement at the many colorful surprises wrapped in each dried husk. It was a moment of grace, when work (even for others) became unexpectedly a joy.

Requests around our home for TV watching or more time at the computer are usually reinforced with the lament, "But I'm BORED!" That line of reasoning seemed to clinch the argument, until I learned some deflecting comebacks. "What's wrong with being bored? Boredom isn't so terrible. It means you have some lovely time on your hands, time to sit back and dream, or be lazy, or make a little effort to launch a new project."

One summer after the initial days of utter and well-earned relaxation, I noticed that time was growing heavy. The children started picking on each other, obviously in need of diversion. What to do? became a major consternation. How does one organize whole days of unplanned minutes? The children need some guidance, I decided. There are things they want to do, but don't have the ability to set long-range goals to make happen. Let's draw up some contracts, I suggested, listing things you want to do anyway and outlining a plan. We'll agree together which activities and how many of each you want to do, and talk about a reasonable reward for fulfilling a mutually designed contract.

The first summer one son's contract included a number of "masterpiece" drawings, reading biographies, memorizing several piano pieces, writing several stories and letters, reading the New Testament, and memorizing some verses. The other son set out to write several poems, construct several three-dimensional figures, read a number of books, compose some tunes for the piano, read a set of Bible story books and memorize some verses.

The next summer there were different lists and different agreements. The contracts weren't fully completed, but certain features received an energetic investment. There was no sense of heavy obligation, since these were voluntary agreements. If other outdoor activities with friends took precedence, that was fine. The contracts were there to channel extra energies in constructive directions.

For one summer's reading we focused on books about real people, heroes of one kind or another. Our list included Fannie Lou Hamer, George Washington Carver, Gandhi, John Wesley, Michelangelo, Tchaikovsky, Mark Twain, Beatrix Potter, Francis of Assisi and stories of Anabaptist martyrs of the sixteenth century. We talk now and again about what makes a true hero, and who some of our heroes are. There are uncles and grandmothers among them. The latest hero is a Slovenian basketball star, featured in *Sports Illustrated*. He played on a prominent American team. Marko Lokar is a devoted pacifist. When he refused to wear an American flag on his uniform during the war in the Persian Gulf, he was heckled and hassled by spectators. There were many insults and even death threats over the phone. He left the team, and with his pregnant wife returned to his home in Italy, near the Slovenian border. An editorial in *The New York Times* asserted, "It is saddening when even a few Americans use the flag as license for persecution. Yet persecution is the word that most captures the trials of Marko Lokar." Even when his own Slovenian people came under attack by Yugoslav federal forces, Lokar said, "My whole family is involved. I have passionate emotions for freedom and will support the Slovenes in any way I can, but I absolutely can never condone war. To do that would be to reject the teachings of Jesus."

What a hero!

It is urgent for parents to reassert a vital moral authority within the home. Too often we ourselves don't have much of a moral leg to stand on. We're confused and vacillating when it comes to questions of lifestyle. We want to provide for our children, to give them every opportunity to thrive. We certainly don't want to come down with heavy rules and "thou shalt not's." And yet the need for gentle, consistent guidance is *more urgent* than ever amid the plethora of enticements.

I know my son at times thinks I'm impossibly stubborn if I don't immediately go out and buy the latest designer sneakers "all his friends are wearing." But there are grace-filled moments too, like when he said, "Mom, I like you. You're not stingy, just careful."

We need other parents to support us in making good decisions with our children. When my child reports, "But Randy's mom lets their kids get (this or that)," I know the pressure is on. The ways our children use us as parents against each other make it imperative to have parent support groups for discerning together what is helpful for our children. If within the church community we can achieve at least a minimal consensus among parents, we empower each other and our children to make wise choices. Somehow, in standing together it becomes easier for everyone—parents and children alike—to resist the temptation to conform. We don't only stand *against* G.I. Joe dolls or the latest fads in clothing and entertainment. We stand together for the fun of it, for intergenerational corn husking, for creative summer fun. We stand together in honoring true heroes who give us courage to stand tall and be counted among those who make the world a more wholesome, delightful place to be.

35.
Singing Songs in a Strange Land

During several of the years we lived in Yugoslavia we drove our two boys to school each day over a narrow, rather perilous road winding through villages and vineyards, uphill and down. The journey was made less taxing by the opportunity to converse and enjoy each other's company. For some months the son of a visiting American scholar joined us. I'll call him "Peter." An obstreperous, loud and unpredictable chap, he often stirred things up in a rather unpleasant manner, both at school and in our carload. It was clear to us that he had some deep-seated behavioral problems, and we tried to relate redemptively to him and his mother. Our boys worried out loud about Peter and how he would continue to make things miserable for himself and others if he didn't learn to relate better to friends. One of us suggested that when they returned to the U.S., his mother and he would do well to get some psychological counseling and deal with the behavioral difficulties.

"I wonder what a psychologist would think of me," Joseph pondered after we stated our suggestion for Peter. "Why?" we asked.

"Because I'm so different."

"What do you mean?" we queried.

"Well, our family is so—religious. And my brother and I don't fight all the time. We often like to play together."

"Anything else?"

"Well—we love each other so much in our family."

"Don't you know any other family like that?" we pursued. In his immediate circle of school friends Joseph clearly felt unique. We quickly reminded him of cousins' families and other friends we knew in other locations that resembled our family in many respects. That didn't change the fact that he'd picked up on some distinctives that marked our family off from many others of his acquaintance in the immediate vicinity.

Noting our differentness, our unique identity, has been an ongoing discussion in our family. We try never to put the emphasis on the negative, like saying we don't have certain items because we can't afford them, or we don't do certain things because we're odd.

We may not be wealthy, nor choose to buy all the gadgets the next family has, but we are rich in so many other ways. Look at what we have together—we're free to be creative, to play with words, songs, rhymes, colors; free to explore the great out-of-doors. With what we watch on TV, what we buy, what we eat, the ways we spend our time, the church and friends we relate to—all of these reflect in some way that we are a people with a unique identity, something worth noting and celebrating.

Many, many children today, surrounded by innumerable toys and the latest designer clothes and hours of mind-numbing television fare, are struggling with a sense that they don't matter much to anyone. Parents have less time than ever to spend with them.

If we can cultivate a family spirit within our homes where children know they have to pitch in to make the family work, where we need their help and want their perspectives, they won't mind belonging to a family that is "different," at least not *that* different. But we will be different in the sense of knowing who we are, knowing that our identity is all caught up in celebrating the Kingdom of God among us.

Last summer after a two-week camping trip along the Great Lakes on our way to Mennonite World Conference in Winnipeg, Manitoba, Gerald and I were exhausted. We arrived at our host's home needing a break to recover from our "vacation." On the day before the conference started our hosts graciously offered to take our three children swimming so Mom and Dad could have some quiet. As we sat reading, we heard a young boy's voice from the neighboring driveway. He rode his bike up and down, singing at the top of his lungs: "Heavenly sunshine, heavenly sunshine, flooding my soul with glory divine. Alleluia, Jesus is mine."

Tears welled up as I moved to the sliding glass door to watch him. We'd learned that the neighbors belong to a small sect called "Wenger Mennonites." They resist many contacts with the outside world and wouldn't be among those attending the large gathering of Mennonite families from around the world at the huge assembly in Winnipeg. There would have been a time when I viewed such sectarian behavior with scorn. Now I pondered it for its strengths.

The boy sang and sang, with complete joy-filled abandon. As his bike wove back and forth, back and forth, our silent praise rose with his melodies, a fervent offering on that sun-filled morning to the great God of the heavens. How many children in other neighborhoods sing with such lusty fervor? No doubt we'd find far more of them playing at Ninja turtles than singing hymns filled with sunshine.

Am I longing for some bygone era, a quaint sectarian community? No!

Singing with our children, reading to them, working beside them, hosting neighbors and friends is never out-of-date. Making our homes places where God and the world and the family of God are celebrated is never quaint! But such a life together must be deliberately cultivated. When we as a called-out people sing our songs in this strange land, it requires an extraordinary fortitude and devotion.

VI.

Grace-Notes at Home

36.
Why Celebrate?

Every day is a most amazing day, if we have eyes to see it, ears to hear it, active senses to wrap around and enter into it. The world is studded and strewn with wonders—acts of unexpected kindness, moments of true companionship, music to touch a deep spot of pain, a story that reveals my story in a new light, the flight of a bird that moves me to worship. Most of us hardly notice, rushing pell-mell toward who knows where. We haven't cultivated worship in tiny moments spread throughout the day; we leave it rather for sanctimonious Sunday mornings. But worship is a daily, moment-by-moment exercise. It is like breathing and knowing with each breath that life is a gift; each moment is wrapped with a ribbon of God's presence.

The alternative to sleepy dullness isn't giddiness. In order to celebrate we don't have to whip up positive vibrations all the time. Cultivating a celebrative lifestyle has nothing to do with the power of positive thinking.

Rather it is holding the fresh spring water in my hands, cupping them so that I can watch it trembling, dripping, before its coolness rushes down my throat. Worship is awakening all our senses to experience life in its fullness.

What more than all else energizes our desire to celebrate? Why do we take time to sing around the breakfast table? Why do we light candles during Advent? Why do we retell the story of our child's birth on her birthday? Why do we pick a bunch of flowers for a friend and prepare a special meal for Thanksgiving? Why do we seek to create a rhythm of meaningful activities in our homes?

It all comes of a love affair with the Creator. It comes of a love that has so profoundly awakened us to newness of life that we ache to respond, we long to celebrate. When the love of God courses through one's being, all of life becomes sacred and every moment is worth savoring because God's love is present in it.

37.
Forgiveness: A Family's Saving Grace

The other evening at the supper table I sensed I had little emotional reserve left to cope with the remaining hours of the day. It had been several weeks of single-parenting, with Gerald off to Eastern Europe on a teaching stint. We had all expected to accompany him, but the political situation heated up before the trip and didn't bode well for assuring the well-being of three children. So I committed myself to managing the home front for a month in his absence, including some ongoing pastoral responsibilities at church and overseeing a major addition to our house. Generally things were going smoothly, but I'd noticed my flash points were easily activated, a sign that the reserves were low.

Spring and summer evenings often beckon us outside to work in the garden, pick raspberries, visit and play with the neighbors. With near-drought conditions, we were forced to water everything that we didn't want to turn various shades of brown. The children usually beg to help with the hose, often teasing each other with spray more than concentrating on the garden. In the middle of conversation with neighbors I heard a fight heating up between my two sons. I turned to see the one who had just received the full brunt of an unprovoked shot of hose water jumping on the perpetrator of the offense. Both proceeded verbally to shoot and counter-shoot about who had done what to spark the spat. The one, drenched from head to toe, stalked off, tearfully yelling his indignation, while the other, totally unrepentant, piled on more verbal abuse. I walked over to the one with the hose, after calling his name evoked no response, and with my arm on his shoulder, quietly but firmly told him how he was out of line with this behavior.

It wasn't much later when I, now with hose in hand, overheard another spat heating up and told the original perpetrator that he must remain at some distance from the other. The pestering was to stop immediately! No sooner had I turned my back, than he made yet another irritating remark that set his brother off again. Now I, in anger, turned the full force of the hose on this, my recalcitrant son. Shock radiated from his face as he sprang away, hurrying inside for water to dump on me. Little sister watched in alarm as Mom lost her cool. She, who so often manages to stir up trouble herself, knew immediately when Mom had crossed the line of normal parental behavior. She proceeded loudly and tearfully to tell me that I should *not* have gotten her brother wet! Humph! I thought; what does a three-year-old know about justice?

I retreated indoors, only to find that the dog had vomited all over the living room rug. After directing the children in no uncertain terms to clean up after *their* dog, I stewed around trying to think clearly again.

Next I sat them all down and walked through the progression of events with them. I apologized for what had seemed an overreaction, explaining as I often have before, that even though I'm Mom, I am not blessed with an unlimited supply of patience. My son didn't appreciate it when I suggested that he had gotten a dose of his own medicine, but begrudgingly resigned himself to allow that perspective eventually.

In further discussion at bedside, we didn't talk much about whether my action was appropriate or not. We hugged each other and prayed together. Even though my patience runs out, I said, my forgiveness and love for each one of you haven't come close to running out. We have tested each other's limits again and found that they are real, but forgiveness also can freely flow once more; love still undergirds.

The ability to be honest about my limits and about my own personal needs even with my children has enhanced their willingness to forgive, extending to me in turn the freedom to be human. A back scratch request from the original scamp put a soft Amen on our bedtime chat, strengthening our bond and fortifying us to survive the next flare-up which will inevitably come, probably tomorrow.

38.
A Moth is a Moth. . .

Our family is cultivating a love for camping, which has been at times a soggy, stubborn struggle with the elements. At home last summer we longed for rain, day after dry day, to water our garden and yard, but it didn't come until it burst out of the heavens with huge fireworks our first night in a tent in West Virginia. The skies then showered us almost daily on our two-week outing.

We took turns keeping spirits undampened, but it was a challenge, especially because Mom and Dad would have headed the expedition home if it were only up to us. In truth, hiking through a rain-drenched forest lent an exceptional eerie loveliness, reminding us of rain forests far away. Under dripping branches the forest was filled with unexpected finds—wild blueberries beside deep dark rocky crevices, ancient gnarled trunks sculpted into striking shapes, sunbeams penetrating through the mist to display myriad shades of green.

Communing with nature brings one close to beauty, yes, but also cruelty. At the source of the Mississippi River, strange cries from the creekbed summoned us—a frog halfway enveloped by the mouth of a snake pled for mercy. The scene evoked cries of protest from a couple of boys, but no mercy from the snake.

There is no end to the ways our lives are interwoven with all of life on this beloved and sometimes brutal earth home, but we're oblivious to most of them. When the wonder and complexity of our world are beyond fathoming, how can we ever allow ourselves to grow calloused and dull? I'm convinced that to nurture the simple virtue of delighting in life is to open a way into the heart of God for our children. One of the strongest defenses we can give them against hopelessness is to celebrate with them the intricacy of God's good earth. The mystery of "how could this be?" opens them to ponder their Creator.

One evening while using the campground restroom, I overheard a young girl say to her adult companion, "Look at that pretty moth!"

Her companion quipped, "Oh, a moth is a moth is a moth."

"But Uncle Bill likes moths!"

Hurrah for Uncle Bill and hurrah for his niece who noticed that a moth is more than a moth.

Evening after evening at different campsites we were regaled by one of the most ethereally lovely birdcalls I have ever heard. We'd searched and searched for the source, all in vain. In the middle of another shower, the call came again. "Please," I begged the boys and their dad, "will someone track it down? I'll give a reward to whoever can discover which bird that is."

The boys lit out with binoculars in hand—disregarding the rain. Their dad followed. They all soon came racing back to report that it was a white-throated sparrow, confirmed by another camper more versed in bird lore.

I was incredulous. A sparrow? Are you sure? For this fledgling bird-watcher, a sparrow was a sparrow was a sparrow. But no more!

One day while our son Joseph splashed in a cove along the Adriatic, a snorkler brought him a sea cucumber, a sea urchin and a beautiful orange starfish to study and adore. He held them, turning them over in his hands and marveling. "May I take them home?" he wondered. "You can take them home and they will die," replied the diver, "or you can leave them here and they will live."

It was a hard choice for a four-year-old, but finally he handed them back to be returned to their salt-sea home.

Our children hear a whole lot today about environmental concerns, endangered species, recycling efforts—much more than I ever did growing up. But all the lecturing in the world won't do what a few encounters with the real world will do to nurture a love, a respect for our earth home. Life is far more than the latest fad, hot car or glittering gadget. Armed with an inquisitive love for adventure, we will find no end of excitement in store, if we are willing to venture forth.

Whether watching stars wheeling overhead while out camping, or relishing the fruits of our love/hate relationship with the garden, the more we open our senses to our world, the more we feel compelled to proclaim with the psalmist, "The heavens declare the glory of God; . . . Their voice goes out into all the earth."

39.
Swinging with Grace

"Rejoice in the Lord always. I will say it again: Rejoice!"
(Philippians 4:4, NIV)

On days when somber, heavily laden skies poured down, drowning some greatly anticipated excursion in rain, my mother used to recite with a teasing sparkle in her eyes, "'Tain't no use to grumble and complain. 'Tis just as cheap and easy to rejoice. When God sorts out the weather and sends us rain, then rain's my choice."

Perhaps it was such statements that awakened an early interest in theology within the tender, unsuspecting folds of my consciousness. Rejoice? When your dearest hopes have been drenched? Is it alright to loudly lament the turn of events? Is God really in the business of ruining vacation plans and expecting me to be happy about it? What an artificial manipulation of feelings! It seems more honest and healthy to have a good cry and commiserate together about how disappointed we all are.

And then we do have a choice. Will we let the rain ruin the whole day, lashing out at other family members, moping in bed, boiling with anger—or can we perhaps redeem the day? Can we pick up the pieces after broken plans, shattered hopes, ruined expectations, or do we remain victims of our circumstances? Are we finally persons completely at the mercy of the circumstances that swirl around us, or are we able to make decisions about how to respond to what comes our way?

Paul writes: "I have learned to be content whatever the circumstances. I know what it is to be in need, and I know what it is to have plenty. I have learned the secret of being content in any and every situation, whether well fed or hungry, whether living in plenty or in want" (Philippians 4:11, 12 NIV).

The man saying this had been through fearsome calamities. He was a person with such conviction and passion that he ran into all kinds of resistance, survived countless beatings, imprisonments, stonings; he spent many sleepless nights in hunger and thirst, in cold and exposure. On Paul's frequent journeys he was in danger from rivers, robbers, and those who hated him. He was repeatedly shipwrecked. And yet he said, "I have learned to be content. " What is Paul's secret?

Paul encountered many of his hardships while on the road, moving in and out of foreign places. The tensions and stresses we live with in our own homes and places of work seem to pale in comparison to his exotic adventures. In fact, we tend to glorify hardships experienced by daring pioneers on distant shores while in the same breath belittling the courage and fortitude it takes to cope with the everyday struggles of ordinary life at home.

One of my greatest fears on returning to the United States after years of service in Europe was that our lives would spiral out of control, that the demands of children, extended family, job, church, ongoing East European ties and all would be impossible to balance with serenity. Home, work and family is a massive juggling act for all of us, one that often defeats us.

Often I imagine that perfect synchronization lies just on the other side of trying a little harder. With an ounce of additional patience or an extra rush of determination I might pull off a magnificent, harmonious juggling act. There are rare moments when I sit back in my chair and bask in the cozy, warm feeling that "we must be doing something right."

But *most* of the time there are too many interruptions, too few moments alone, too many errands, too many unfinished tasks, too many arguments, too much anxiety, too much complaining . . .

A wise friend of mine remarked, "I'm convinced that life is always a bit off-keel. There's always too much of something. If you're married, there's too much of marriage. If you're single, there's too much aloneness. If you have a job there's too much of it. If you're at home there's too much of that."

The myth of the perfectly balanced life haunts the recesses of our consciousness. Somewhere in intangible space an heroic person embodies the ideal mix of solitude and friendship, recreation and work, family and church life in perfect proportion—an idyllic marvel.

My life always seems off-balance. I've thought sometimes of the Foucault pendulum, swinging first to one side, returning to center only to swing far to the other side. Even with heroic effort I can't remain in that perfectly aligned centered spot. And yet ironically there is a certain balance achieved by swinging first one way and then allowing oneself to be tugged back. I often feel off-balance, and yet in my imbalance there is (I'm beginning to believe) a kind of balance. The secret to the pendulum's ability to maintain an equilibrium (and not just a haphazard bouncing back and forth) is the cable attached to a fixed point at the top of the dome.

Back to Paul and the secret of being content. The secret to maintaining a calm confidence at the center of things isn't ultimately dependent on the circumstances around us, he implies. Our peace isn't dependent on the constancy of relationships that impact our lives. What Paul is reassuring us is that there is a source of peace and inner strength that is unrelated to and unaffected by all that would throw us off balance. Like the pendulum attached by a cable to the ceiling, we are free, when in touch with our fixed point, to swing back and forth, to err and correct our swing, to remain off-balance while essentially being in balance. There is stability and dynamism in this image. We swing in response to events and people in our days, but we are secure in a central relationship with Jesus Christ.

As long as our lifeline remains firmly connected to the Source of all life, the chances are good that we can learn from all seasons. We can rejoice even in times of profound difficulty. Despite all the troublesome things that happen to us, the stress of work and twisting of relationships that throw our swing way off balance, there is that central relationship that tugs us back toward center once again. That love relationship with Christ, at the core, is a central affiliation around which all else can be balanced.

40.
"Run Come See What This River Has Done!"

Steve Goodman died of leukemia in Chicago in the mid-1980s. He was a well-known singer/songwriter. One of his most popular songs began, "Riding on the City of New Orleans, Illinois Central, Monday morning blues. . ." Steve never stooped to the mindless platitudes of popular patriotism to make his songs work, but he built into many of them a genuine love for this land, its people, and its remarkable geography. One of his best songs expresses his wonderment at the phenomenal grandeur of the Colorado River etching its way through centuries and aeons of rock in the Grand Canyon. It's entitled, "Run come see what this river has done!"

We spent some time at the Grand Canyon this summer. What the river has done is truly beyond imagining. We learned that in the last six million years, the river has cut down through two billion years of earth's geological history. The black rock of the canyon's Inner Gorge is some of the oldest exposed rock on this planet. The canyon is like an open storybook of geological history. There are some 21 layers of sedimentary rock exposed. In the top limestone layer alone there is evidence of the advance and retreat of at least seven seas, one Sahara-like desert and several lagoons.

The marvel for us was that this phenomenal canyon spread out before us was accomplished through the process of decay and erosion—terms not usually associated with grandeur and beauty. The river flows in ancient patterns down amid even more ancient rocks, yet the river itself is new in every flashing moment.

The contrast of vibrant newness splashing against unfathomable oldness and the contrast of something so splendid wrought from such destruction sent our minds flowing toward analogies. In some ways, the Colorado River is like the vibrant, ever-changing story of our faith, a faith that has carved its way through millennia of our human experience.

The river serves as a picture of God's action in human history. Relentlessly it wears down through the layers of civilization, both creating and destroying as it goes. It carries away great amounts of material, while also revealing unexpected beauty in the parts that are tough enough to endure.

Amid much erosion and destruction, the river flows on. Its very vitality defies decay and death. From the rim it is possible to survey the vast splendor of canyon and river. For those willing to struggle down through the rough shattered terrain of the canyon to the leaping river itself, daring to jump on a raft and ride on its boiling cascades, there is endless adventure. The movement of the people of God and of all creation toward the final culmination of all things is dynamic. To abandon oneself to its flow is dangerous, but there is nothing so exhilarating!

This is a troubling word picture, inasmuch as it is built around the continual process of erosion and disintegration. Is God presiding over a universe that is gradually running down to nothing? Absolute zero?

Perhaps. But if the Grand Canyon is a testimonial, the beauty wrought by a Master Craftsman, even out of decay and breakdown, is without compare. And the white flashing waters roll on toward eternity. That something as splendid as the Grand Canyon could come out of something as destructive as erosion heralds a dauntless hope. What could be more comforting than to know that our God is the kind of God who can take what could destroy us and transform it into a work of indescribable beauty?

41.
Home at Last

Weeks before school's end our boys were counting the days. It wasn't that they hated school or were doing poorly. There were no nagging grievances that one could put a finger on. The last day of school simply meant release from a regimented life dictated by the panic before the arrival of the school bus and its dragging trip home midafternoon.

At bedtime shortly after the glorious advent of summer holidays, after lounging lazily all day with a new book and playing a long game with Dad, Timothy leaped into my arms, squeezed me with exuberance shining from his face, and then danced round and round with joy radiating from every pore in his body. "It's really summer vacation!" he laughed, hardly believing his good fortune. "There's nothing I *have* to do."

His unbridled delight evoked memories of my childhood trips home after weeks away at boarding school in Ethiopia. Waking up on the first morning of a holiday break, in my own bed, in my own room—home at last—a memory of sublime joy! No wake-up bells, no negotiating with roommates over cleaning chores in preparation for morning inspection, no rushing to beat the bell for breakfast or first class. Only the lullaby of the wind whistling through the window screen, welcoming me home.

Is there any more profound joy? No bed has ever felt more comfortable. No four walls have ever felt more secure. No wind singing through the window screen has ever wafted a sweeter music—a tune of sabbath rest in a fond, familiar place.

A season of rest. An *attitude* of rest. If there is a quality that most characterizes at-homeness, it is *rest*. We used to sing, "There is a place of quiet rest, near to the heart of God." Another old hymn came powerfully to mind as I faced into the birth of our third child after an urgent, eleventh-hour flight to Pennsylvania from Yugoslavia: "Jesus, I am resting, resting in the joy of what thou art. I am finding out the greatness of thy loving heart."

An attitude of rest. In a day when no matter who you talk to there is *never* enough time, cultivating an attitude of rest is the only way to survive the pressures with any semblance of serenity. Gone are the days of childhood abandon. The web of obligations, responsibilities, expectations is woven so tightly that we never cut loose and jump with effortless exuberance into the arms of our mother. Gone are the leisurely mornings when we sank deeper into the pillow's softness because we were home at last. But there is the voice of one who said, "Come to me all you who are weary and burdened, and I will give you rest" (Matthew 11:28 NIV).

When a small local congregation, caught in a deepening crisis, invited Gerald and me to consider serving as co-pastors, my spirit rose to the challenge, yet part of me shrank back. More time demands, more obligations? No thanks. I'd rather not. The words that came to mind as I prayed and reflected were Jesus' own: "Take my yoke upon you and learn from me, for I am gentle and humble in heart, and you will find rest for your soul. For my yoke is easy and my burden is light" (Matthew 11:29-30 NIV). A lovely coincidence: the symbol dominating the front of this congregation's meeting room is a beautifully carved yoke.

Jesus' words appear to be a flagrant contradiction. Carrying a yoke, pulling a heavy plow through clods of soil, is anything but restful. If he had said, "Come to my hammock and learn from me," we'd have joined the leisure club long ago.

The genius of Jesus' imagery is that intuitively we identify with his yoke far more readily than we do with swinging in a hammock.

Growing up means learning to shoulder yokes of every size and shape. Jesus invites us to carry *his* yoke, implying that there is something essentially different about the character of that yoke—so different in fact that we carry it with ease; so different that we know *rest* even while walking beneath its weight. Partnering with One whose shoulders support most of the weight in the yoke we carry together is the secret of learning to know rest every single day.

When Jesus wanted to comfort his disciples, he didn't send a card or bake a cake or recommend therapy. Jesus said, *"Come to me . . . and I will give you rest."* He also did many tangible acts of kindness and miraculous works of healing and feeding. But Jesus' most profound and enduring invitation was, *"Come to me."*

With a compelling picture of comfort Jesus reassured his disciples: "Do not let your hearts be troubled. . . . In my Father's house there are many dwelling places. . . . And if I go and prepare a place for you, I will come again and will take you to myself, so that where I am, there you may be also" (John 14:1-3, NRSV).

"Take you to myself." Home at last!

To rest in Jesus' companionship, whether in the center of the storm, while carrying his yoke, or forever in the Father's house, is truly to come home.

"There would I find a settled rest," wrote Isaac Watts, "while others go and come; no more a stranger, nor a guest, but like a child at home."

Readings and Sources

Achtemeier, Elizabeth. *The Committed Marriage.*
   Philadelphia: Westminster Press, 1976.
Achtemeier, Elizabeth. *Preaching About Family Relationships.*
   Philadelphia: Westminster Press, 1987.
Berger, Brigitte and Peter L. Berger. *The War Over the Family.*
   Garden City, NY: Anchor Press/Doubleday, 1983.
Bly, Robert. *Iron John.*
   Reading, MA: Addison-Wesley, 1990.
Boyer, Ernest. *Finding God at Home.*
   San Francisco: Harper & Row, 1988.
Bronfenbrenner, Urie. "Report of Forum 15—Children and Parents:
   Together in the World," in *Report to the President: White
   House Conference on Children.* (Washington DC: Government
   Printing Office, 1970); cited in Donald Joy, *Parents, Kids and
   Sexual Integrity.*
Dittes, James E. *The Male Predicament.*
   San Francisco: Harper & Row, 1985.
Foster, Richard. *Freedom of Simplicity.*
   San Francisco: Harper & Row, 1971.
Goldberg, Herb. *The New Male.*
   New York: William Morrow, 1979.

Joy, Donald. *Bonding.*
Dallas: Word Publishing, 1985.
Joy, Donald and Robbie Joy. *Lovers— Whatever Happened to Eden?*
Waco, TX: Word Books, 1987.
Joy, Donald. *Rebonding.*
Waco, TX: Word Books, 1989.
Joy, Donald. *Parents, Kids and Sexual Integrity.*
Waco, TX: Word Books, 1988.
Kamerman, Sheila. *Parenting In An Unresponsive Society.*
New York: The Free Press, 1980.
McGinnis, James and Kathleen. *Parenting for Peace and Justice: Ten Years Later.*
Mary Knoll, NY: Orbis Books, 1990.
Miller, John W. *Biblical Faith and Fathering.*
New York: Paulist Press, 1989.
Newsweek Special Edition: "The 21st Century Family."
New York: Newsweek, Inc., Winter/Spring 1990.
Osborne, Philip. *Parenting for the '90s.*
Intercourse, PA: Good Books, 1989.
Ruether, Rosemary Radford. *Sexism and Godtalk.*
Boston: Beacon Press, 1983.
Shenk, Sara Wenger. *Why Not Celebrate!*
Intercourse, PA: Good Books, 1987.
Sider, Ronald. *Completely Pro-Life.*
Downers Grove, IL: InterVarsity Press, 1987.
Spencer, Aida Besancon. *Beyond the Curse.*
Nashville: Thomas Nelson, 1985.
Stevens, Paul. *Marriage Spirituality.*
Downers Grove, IL: InterVarsity Press, 1989.
Visser 't Hooft, W. A. *The Fatherhood of God in an Age of Emancipation.* Philadelphia: Westminster, 1982.
Wangerin, Walter Jr. *The Manger is Empty.*
San Francisco: Harper & Row, 1989.

About the Author

Sara Wenger Shenk spent her childhood in Ethiopia, the daughter of Mennonite missionary educators. In 1975 she graduated from Eastern Mennonite College with a B.A. in English Education. After seminary studies she returned overseas, this time to Yugoslavia with her husband Gerald Shenk. During nearly nine years in Yugoslavia, Sara wrote regular columns for local church publications, often on marriage and family themes.

Sara and Gerald have two sons and a daughter. The sometimes traumatic years of adjusting to motherhood gave rise to her first book, *And Then There Were Three: An Ode to Parenthood*. Further reflection on the spirit of life at home gave rise to her second book, *Why Not Celebrate!*

Sara has a masters degree in Theological Studies from Garrett-Evangelical Theological Seminary in Evanston, Illinois. She currently lives in Harrisonburg, Virginia, where Gerald teaches at Eastern Mennonite Seminary. She serves as pastor of Immanuel Mennonite Church and frequently provides resource to weekend retreats.